FOOTHILLS OF THE FELLS

Foothills of the Fells

Frank Goddard

Photographs by Geoffrey Berry

ROBERT HALE · LIMITED

© *Frank Goddard 1981*

First published in Great Britain 1981

ISBN 0 7091 9341 6

Robert Hale Limited
Clerkenwell House
Clerkenwell Green
London EC1R 0HT

Photoset by Rowland Phototypesetting Limited
Printed in Great Britain by
St Edmundsbury Press, Bury St Edmunds, Suffolk
Bound by Weatherby Woolnough

CONTENTS

ILLUSTRATIONS

8 *Foothills of the Fells*

Black Combe from the shore at Silecroft
Near the summit of Whiteside Pike, Selside
Sadgill, Longsleddale
The Helvellyn Dods from Souther Fell
Binsey with Skiddaw
Raven Crag above Thirlmere's dam
Castle Crag, early British fort above Thirlmere
Silver How from Grasmere's island
Haystacks from Warnscale Bottom
The head of Swindale, looking towards Selside Pike
Old survey device on Branstree above Haweswater

MAP

TO SARAH

INTRODUCTION

This book has had an incubation period of eight years. That is the age of my daughter, Sarah, and until she danced into our family circle my fell-walking life had a tendency to be concerned with the higher fells—not entirely to the exclusion of the foothills, but the Scafells, Gable, Helvellyn and the rest of the big boys usually provided the main course. Sarah shifted the balance as far as family outings were concerned. We started to look at the little hills with a more critical eye and as soon as it became possible to take her on the fells we began to seek out more and more of the mountain midgets and to revisit those that had been ignored for several years.

Taking a toddler on the fells makes a marvellous difference to one's appreciation of the foothills. When your staple diet has been the major mountains and extended days of long mountain walks it is too easy to dash up and down a foothill in an hour or so and say you have "done it" when you have done nothing of the sort. You have just scratched the surface. Make no mistake, the midgets are full of really interesting corners just waiting to be explored and appreciated, if only you can slow your pace and apply a little critical attention. A youngster makes you walk slowly. My wife and I found ourselves spending as much time on a little hill as we would normally devote to a 3,000 footer.

So in part this book is due to Sarah, but a good cross-section of the fells described are still awaiting her attention. There is no need to make a child your excuse for climbing the little hills of Lakeland and indeed they have a great deal to offer for young and old, and for those hardy mortals in their fell-walking prime—if only they can tear themselves away from the giants to sample the joys of the foothills. Some of the fells in the book are well known to regular walkers and even occasional visitors; some are inevitable stepping-stones to the high fells and are climbed as a matter of course on ridge-walking expeditions. Others are little known and unsung but still have the flavour of the real Lakeland about them and it is surprising how often you can walk alone even in high season when the popular paths are taking a beating from countless boots.

By definition a foothill is a minor hill at the base of a higher range and for the purposes of this book that definition is largely true. But readers may question some of my selections. The Howgill Fells are a case in point. It seems odd that the opening chapter of a book entitled *Foothills of the Fells* should be devoted to a group of fells that forms a naturally complete range. I have tried to justify their inclusion by describing them as foothills of the Cumbrian Mountains proper, but their true function in this context is to point to the perils—and pleasures—of the fells in winter. You can meet hazards on any hill at any time but winter walking is something special and experiences on the Howgills can be translated to any of the succeeding chapters. It just happens that my winter walking has usually been among the high tops and the midgets have generally been summer-time hills reserved for the occasional off-day or an outing with my wife and daughter. So a chapter on the Howgills seems a satisfactory way of indicating an extreme of mountain weather that remains true of any hill in Lakeland—and anyway, the Howgills are not all that high. Their summit—The Calf—stands at 2,219 feet but from nowhere do you have as much as 2,000 feet of ascent to contend with in reaching this highest point.

This brings me to the question of qualifications for inclusion. The original idea was to exclude anything of 2,000 feet or more but I soon decided that such a plan was too arbitrary. There are so many fells slightly in excess of this figure that are undeniably foothills according to definition, many of them fells of real character which it would be a pity to leave out. Therefore a secondary qualification had to be found. I hit on the idea of restricting my choice to those hills needing an ascent of no more than 2,000 feet between the lowest point of access and the summit.

Having settled upon this criterion I applied it to my provisional list of seventy-four hills and found that it satisfied every case but one—Seat Sandal. So should Seat Sandal be omitted or should I ignore my chosen qualification and allow it space? Certainly Seat Sandal is a foothill of the Helvellyn/Fairfield group. Granted this premise there is no adequate reason to deny it a place in these pages. And anyway, if you make the rules yourself surely you have the right to bend them a little? Therefore, in goes Seat Sandal, the only exception to the rule—though Ullock Pike comes close to joining it. From Bassenthwaite you have to climb just about 2,000 feet to reach the summit. The original list has been modified and some of the selections have been restricted to a brief mention of a paragraph or so but, apart from Seat Sandal and Ullock Pike, everything else is well within the set limits.

So here are descriptions of a selection of minor Lake District fells—minor in terms of height—leavened by a little personal experience. It could be said that this is an ordinary fell walker's account of some ordinary walking on pleasant little hills. Yet another book about Lakeland? Maybe, but if you have bought it, if you are reading this, then no further justification is needed. And if I can convey just a little of my enthusiasm for my favourite pastime and perhaps encourage a few walkers to try something else and provide some small relief for the heavily populated tracks, it is all to the good. If anyone feels aggrieved that some favourite quiet corners may be popularized, let them rest at ease. In spite of a constant flow of books about the fells there is little sign of any disastrous influx of walkers in any of the out-of-the-way spots that have been discussed. The majority of visitors continues to congregate in the same old places and elsewhere there is still plenty of room for the more selective of us to be absorbed without detriment to the environment. I can still guarantee to find quietude even on the busiest of Bank Holiday weekends.

I must express my gratitude to Mr W. R. Mitchell, editor of the popular Lake District monthly *Cumbria*, and to Roger Smith, editor of *The Great Outdoors*, for allowing me to use and develop material which has previously appeared in their excellent magazines. And a special thank you is due to Geoffrey Berry for agreeing to provide the illustrations. You can hardly pick up a book dealing with the Lake District that does not feature Mr Berry's name among the pictorial credits. This is an instance of quantity going hand in hand with quality and I feel privileged to be able to draw on this valuable source for photographs to enhance these pages.

Finally, let me acknowledge a debt to my wife, daughter and friends who have shared many walks with me—and to my wife for allowing me out on my own to enjoy an occasional spot of solitude on the fells! They say pleasures shared are pleasures doubled. This is undoubtedly true, but there are times when we all like to get away from it all to be alone with our thoughts in the empty hills. There is no better place for indulging this selfish whim than on the fells of Lakeland.

Frank Goddard

1

FIRST FOOT
(Winter in the Howgill Fells)

The year 1976 started cold and crisp and on the first day of January there was no doubt that ours was the "first foot" on the western side of the peaceful Howgill Fells. There was no other boot-print to blemish the thin rendering of snow that covered the grassy slopes. We were hardly surprised. Comparatively few strangers turn towards these lonely fells and even in summer the most usual approach is from the south, from Sedbergh. On this wintry day the smooth flanks were hidden beneath a white tegument; the sheet was clean, the New Year was upon us and a silent solitude gripped the hills. Even the sheep were conspicuously absent, enjoying the fleshpots of the intakes because of the prevailing conditions on high. Only the Black Horse o' Busha' was out and about up there but that is an inanimate creature, a fortuitous arrangement of scree below the ridge of Bush Howe looking more like a camel than a horse and though it was etched in white the outline remained clear enough to be visible—if you knew where to look. It appeared to have taken to ermine.

There were three of us but my wife and daughter soon turned back. Junior was far too young to be on the tops in winter, especially with more snow likely, but she enjoyed the walk to the foot of the long incline of White Fell. Since then she has reached the O.S. column on The Calf—in summer—striding out with an enthusiasm that caused dad to look to his laurels. But January snow brings a transformation, even on low ground, so that what would be an easy afternoon stroll in July can become a formidable undertaking for unprepared walkers.

Gossamer-soft flakes began to drift out of the gathering gloom of a snow-laden sky. Persistent but not physically unpleasant in the valley, this spoke of a steady accumulation that would isolate the lonely farmsteads and add to the problems of local inhabitants, but bring joy to children who would have sport on their doorsteps. On the tops it could be a different matter, and so it proved. I stepped out of calm, snow-filled air into the onslaught of an icy gale which made the problem of remaining upright more significant than the effort of ploughing through a foot or more of freshly deposited powder. Visibility was virtually nil and the obvious course for a solitary walker in a complete white-out was a prompt return. Indeed, I overshot the summit ridge and floundered on slopes that could only be the head of Red Gill Beck, the stream that makes a dramatic entry into the lowland scene as Cautley Spout at the wrong side of the Howgills.

The intention had been to follow the summer tourist route from The Calf down to Sedbergh. Now even the idea of seeking out the O.S. column was ludicrous. It might have been only half a dozen strides away but in the all-enveloping swirl of a polar blizzard that left me feeling like Oates marching to his doom the only chance of locating the pillar would be by walking into it. The complicated geography of the Howgills is confusing without snow in this abundance and for some moments there was real doubt about my position. A belatedly produced compass helped me re-cross the watershed, down to Castley by way of Bram Rigg—not the way up, but good enough in the circumstances. I would be content to reach Sedbergh by road. As it happened my wife judged the conditions with accuracy and met me half-way—with barely a moment to spare. It was a shovel and sand job to get out and I suspect another quarter hour would have seen us both walking.

The Howgill Fells are a complete mountain system in themselves and though the highest point stands at only 2,219 feet the ridges, particularly in the northern half, are long enough and similar enough to make this a place to treat with respect. You need to navigate with confidence when mist curtains the view. These fells have their own distinctive character. Sandwiched between the magnificent fell country of Lakeland and the wild moorlands of the

Pennines, they belong to neither. Smooth, grassy ridges
are flanked by steep slopes where sheep and fell ponies
happily graze. Lacking the tarns and crags of typical
mountain country they nevertheless contrive to look like
mountains, especially under snow. When winter tightens
its grip they can present hazards to compare with any
highland region and should never be underestimated.
Given the right conditions there is some fine ski-ing
country here, but unfortunately their modest stature
means that the snow does not usually linger. You have to
take the chance when it is offered.

The Howgills are easily reached from the tourist centres
of southern Lakeland. They are only a short drive from
Kendal and so are often regarded as part of the Lake
District fells. The National Park boundary follows the old
A6 over Shap Fell so walkers who regularly frequent the
area in all seasons may think of these hills as a bonus,
beyond Lakeland proper but near enough to provide an
alternative when they fancy a change of scene. The group
has always been neglected as a walkers' playground and
even now, with increasing pressure on our resources, it is
outside the tourist net. You can often walk alone here
when the major Lakeland valleys seem filled to the brim
with folk on foot or awheel. Even The Calf, the highest
point, may be neglected when Helvellyn's summit resembles opening day at the sales. Yet the Howgills are
receiving more attention nowadays. The building of the
M6 motorway has opened up new views for motorists who
see in their windscreens a shop-window of soaring hills, all
looking much higher than the reality. Decked in snow this
is a scene of almost alpine splendour, a ready-made
advertisement that must in time bring more visitors to a
land that has so much to offer the genuine hill walker.

Though the Lake District National Park makes no demand in this direction the Yorkshire Dales National Park
claims a good half of the group. The Dales Park coincides
with the limits of the old Yorkshire West Riding hereabouts. The boundary takes in Cautley Spout, passes over
The Calf, then ranges north to follow Carlin Gill to the
River Lune. North of this line the Howgills once belonged

to Westmorland but now all this land is within the new county of Cumbria.

Sedbergh is the natural centre for anyone who wishes to explore the area. With a wealth of fine upland country in the neighbourhood there is plenty to occupy any dedicated walker for quite a while. Yorkshire's Three Peaks are within easy striking distance of anyone with a car and to the east are the wild heights of upper Swaledale and Wensleydale. Dentdale and Garsdale are on the doorstep. But the Howgills must rank supreme in the Sedbergh scene. It may be that they lack the craggy excitement of Lakeland, and certainly the highest point is little more than two-thirds the height of Scafell Pike. In addition to The Calf there is a cluster of other tops that raise their heads above the 2,000-foot contour. Calders, Great Dummacks, Bram Rigg Top, Bush Howe, Hare Shaw and Fell Head can all be visited in a simple stroll without much loss of height. Further east are Yarlside and Randygill Top, standing slightly aloof from the main group.

The usual name given to this compact group of fells may be something of a mystery unless you take the trouble to study the map in some detail. The "Sedbergh Fells" would seem a more obvious choice, you might think. Yet at the south-west corner of this mini-mountain system are a few houses strung along a minor road which go by the name of Howgill. Though well sign-posted on the road west out of Sedbergh this hamlet and parish are even less known than their namesake fells. But whatever the name, it is all fine walking country for those who like the freedom of the hills. Above the intakes there are no walls to break the stride, though a fence does reach up to the ridge of Calders. Not many really positive ways have been trodden out and the few that do exist hardly scar the fellsides like some of our more popular mountain tracks. A complete traverse on a north-south axis makes a good expedition of some ten miles, summer or winter, but you do need to be sure of your transport at either end of the route.

The overall impression is that the Howgill Fells are all grass, but this is not strictly true. There is fine ravine scenery at Black Force, a tributary of Carlin Gill. On the

other side of the range is the splendid cliff of Cautley Crag,
but it is not the sort of place to attract rock climbers—or so
it would seem to one who has had only passing acquaintance with the sport. The crags are too broken and would
not present a serious, continuous climb even if the rock
was stable enough for safe climbing, which is doubtful. Yet
the place provides an exciting panorama, a wide sweep of
dramatic verticality in what is really a fell-walkers' preserve. With Cautley Spout to add a dash of spice this combe
is the one place that attracts tourists in search of the
spectacular. You can stroll to the foot of the cascades
without much effort—and take grandma along too.

In February 1978 grandma would not have appreciated
the trip. With the country in the grip of one of the most
outstanding cold spells in years she would have found even
the first few icy steps from the road to the footbridge over
the River Rawthey a hazardous undertaking. Yet for well-
equipped hill walkers the conditions were really superb
and the day I chose proved ideal. The omens were good. A
clear blue sky was occasionally decorated by swiftly moving patches of cumulus. East-facing slopes glistened in
their covering of hard-packed snow, spelling out the importance of an ice axe as an essential implement. It would
be cold, yes, with a sharp, biting wind sweeping the tops,
but this was going to be a day to remember.

Cautley Spout was festooned in ice, great bulbous pipes
of it with water singing a subdued song somewhere in the
depths. A couple of ravens drifted casually over the ravine
to alight on the slopes of Yarlside and strut with perky
assurance where the pale, starved grasses showed through
the snow high on the south-facing slope. They were to
reappear at intervals as constant companions, like
wardens overlooking my progress. To the left was Cautley
Crag. From this angle the cliff looked vast—like a
Cinerama screen viewed from a seat too near the front of
the stalls. Cliffs always look so much more impressive
when set in contrasting surroundings and on this day the
contrast was even more pronounced. Though the usual
setting of grass was hidden under a cloak of snow the
hinterland remained smooth, emphatically so, and the

normally dark rock took on an ebony hue against the winter whiteness. Nature was staging her own brand of theatre, a dramatic extravaganza on the grand scale with each element in the scene etched with sharp clarity in the clear, frosty air. This was truly a time to stand and stare.

An increase in height revealed the long trough of Bowderdale stretching impressively to the north from the distinctive pass at its head. From here to the flattened acres of the summit plateau the snow lay in untold depths, blown from above and packed hard by persistent winds and frost. It was like walking on a tilted beach with the ripples of a receding tide frozen in time so that the spike of an ice axe used for balance made little impression on the icy surface. Red Gill Beck and its tributaries, the headwaters of Cautley Holme Beck, carve deep watercourses down these gentle slopes between The Calf and Cautley Crag. Now the northern slopes of these gills sported huge curling cornices, boldly carved sculptures of which Henry Moore might well have been proud. Elsewhere the snowy ripples had become storm-tossed waves held immobile like glacial ghosts. Steeper slopes above held loose powder suspended dangerously on the frozen crust, waiting for a careless foot to start the slide into the deep hollow.

There was less snow on the summit, but plenty of ice. I had thought that I might possibly have had the place to myself in mid-week but a couple of figures with a dog were to be seen departing towards Calders. The resident ravens were in occupation too, but they took to the air and disappeared towards Cautley. I leaned against the O.S. column and looked west across the Lune valley to the far fells of the Lake District. Decked in snow they held a promise of great things for those who could find the time to scale those winter heights. The Coniston group showed well and ranging away to the right was the long white line of the High Street tops. Between and beyond these hills was a bank of cloud, or so it seemed until sudden recognition resolved the distant shape into the jumble of peaks around the Scafells, with the gap of Mickledore quite easy to place, and all looking so much higher than imagination could possibly suspect.

There was plenty of wind and no shelter on the flat top of The Calf, and the immediate surroundings were as smooth and glassy as an ice rink. It was no place to open out the lunch packet so I turned towards Calders in the hope of finding a suitable spot there. First impressions suggested little improvement, but the tops of the fence posts poked above the snow and gave rise to an idea. I stepped over the fence to carve a neat bucket seat in the frozen bank, lagged it with my waterproofs, and settled in comfort with just my head above the snow. An ice axe can be useful in more ways than one might suspect!

"This is the life," I thought. The sun shone on my face, the wind raced by just above my head, and away in the distance Ingleborough's proud outline showed between my outstretched feet. The nearer Yorkshire hills lay like great iced monsters on all sides. Wild Boar Fell and Baugh Fell were particularly imposing across the intervening valley, with gullies like gnarled fingers reaching up to claw the skyline. Here was the perfect situation in which to enjoy a well-earned snack in the undisturbed peace of the winter hills. I poured steaming coffee from a flask and raised the welcome cup to my lips.

And then it happened. With a roar like a demented banshee a jet aeroplane drilled a tunnel of sound through the air a couple of hundred feet above my head, swung into view and dived past my feet into the Rawthey valley, far below. As the echoes reverberated across the fell, apparently in one ear and out of the other and performing agonizing corkscrews between, the plane described a wide arc and eased itself over Baugh Fell to disappear in the direction of Wensleydale and disturb the inhabitants there. Gazing wistfully at the coffee stains I reflected that the R.A.F. seem to regard me as fair game. On the remote wastes of Mungrisdale Common at the back of Blencathra—as lonely a spot as it is possible to find in Lakeland—another playful pilot once performed the same trick and, more recently, as we climbed out of Newlands to the summit of Dale Head yet one more member of the modern air force enjoyed his fun.

My route of descent led over Great Dummacks and

round the southern rim of Cautley Crag. A convex slope of snow packed like concrete encouraged careful progress, out of the sun and into the icy shade. My companions of the fell, the friendly ravens, rose on my right and swung away to vanish amidst the black recesses of Cautley Crag calling a cheerful farewell "Cronk" as they passed, and within half an hour I was leaning on the Rawthey footbridge. The ice-encrusted banks of the river were evidence of the hard life of the local hill farmers whose sheep were penned in nearby intakes, but for one who uses the hills for recreation this had been an indescribably beautiful day of snow and ice, of sun and clear blue sky. I watched a couple of wrens flirting along the river bank, two of our tiniest birds to compare with those ravens up aloft, and reflected happily on one of the finest of short winter walks.

2

STARTING THEM YOUNG
(Walking with a Toddler)

The Howgill Fells in winter can be representative of the fell walker's ideal of hill country at its best. However, the walking described in the preceding chapter is in sharp contrast to the main theme of this book, which is generally concerned with easy walking on small hills, where family groups may enjoy their leisure without making too drastic a demand upon stamina and energy. The summer Howgills are an easier proposition and though distances can be long the total altitude to be climbed, even to the highest summit, never approaches 2,000 feet for you have a built-in start of some 500 feet from the lowest starting points. Some of the hills featured in later chapters have ascents well in excess of this. Perhaps the Howgills are, strictly speaking, not so much foothills as a foothill group—when compared with the mountains of Lakeland. Yet even the smallest of foothills can be a very serious undertaking in severe weather and that is sufficient reason for a preliminary chapter which highlights the dangers and delights of the fells in winter. And even summer can provide the unexpected. I have walked in a couple of feet of snow on Grasmoor in June—the day after meeting with a miniature blizzard on modest Latrigg. The moral is simple. Never underestimate the hills in any season of the year.

A more likely summer hazard is rain which, in combination with wind, can be just as serious as snow, and Britain's favourite holiday month is far too often guilty in this respect. We English have a touching belief that August is synonymous with summer. Repeated disillusionment does little to dispel the idea and on those occasions when belief and fact coincide, rather than being treated as exceptions which highlight the norm, serve only to underline the basic misconception that our eighth month is the hottest.

On one of those rather special days when August donned its finest guise and almost tropical sunshine prevailed we climbed to the summit of Loughrigg by one of those devious routes that make the place a delight. We probably took longer to reach the top that day than ever before. Certainly, Scafell Pike could have been climbed and we would have had the return journey well under way by the time we reached Loughrigg's highest point at 1,101 feet. I remember spending a careless half hour watching the contents of my tobacco pouch dry out on a convenient rock after accidental immersion in a minor beck.

The top was crowded, as usual, so we strolled across to the eastern summit in search of reasonable privacy. The place was occupied. A pair of proud parents had spread a travelling blanket over the turf and baby was crawling about on it, gurgling happily while mum was engaged in photographing its efforts. On inquiry we discovered that the child was seven months old. Dad was relaxing beside the tableau, radiating paternal pride, as well he might considering the healthy appearance of his son and heir. His rest was well earned for it was he who had provided the motive power that had brought the youngster from Ambleside. At the time we were quietly surprised but the incident was mentally filed away until the time was ripe for my wife and me to consider such problems for ourselves.

When the course of events introduced a daughter to our household this youngest member of the family curtailed our walking exploits. Although I was still able to indulge in long walks the question of conscience entered into the matter and before long we purchased one of those papoose-type kiddy carriers that are so often seen on the backs of parents nowadays. After all, it is only fair to keep the family together when mother enjoys the outdoors too. Willing though she may be to accept the role of baby-sitter when dad wants to take to the fells, too ready an acceptance of such good-natured wifely tolerance could lead to family friction in time.

The new order meant a reappraisal of the Lakeland fells and we soon came to realize the merits of the smaller hills that we had tended to neglect. We began to tick off a collection of lesser heights, hills that had repeatedly been set aside for off-days, or the time when ageing limbs might make the longer walks less of a joy than at present. Of course, some of these mini-mountains had always been a part of our staple diet but we soon came to realize that the eagerness which had so often taken us over the high fells had caused us to miss a great deal of pleasure. Some of the unconsidered foothills proved to be lesser only in terms of altitude. Often they turned out to be real gems, many of them far superior to comparative giants in interest and scenery. The birth of our daughter opened the door to much fine country that in our ignorance we had passed by in the headlong rush to the skyline.

Of course, a major consideration was now the comfort and feelings of the young one. Taking a very young child on such outings, even a simple ramble through gentle countryside, is not just a case of packing her on your back and treating her as so much extra luggage. A child is a living being and, because of youth, is the most important member of the party. With such thoughts in mind I feel it could be of value to readers with similar problems if a few notes relating to our own experiences in walking with a toddler were to be included here. What use experience, if not shared? If parents decide that this is not how they would do it there will have been gain, even if negative in nature. However, if these ideas are not relevant to your own situation by all means turn to Chapter 3.

At every stage in our walks our actions and intentions were governed by answers to the question, "How is the youngster going to be affected?" Remember that while you are generating heat through exercise, the more so for the extra weight carried, the child is passive. (Her hands are not, though, and my hair has taken a lot of punishment. No one really accepts this as a valid reason for my thinning thatch, but that's my story and I'm sticking to it!) Though the weather may be ideal from your own point of view as an active walker your passenger is likely to lose body heat quite rapidly unless effectively clothed. Even ample clothing is no guarantee for warmth. The first time we took Sarah out we walked only about a mile but we were surprised to discover how cold she became in the short time we were away from the car.

We quickly realized that the answer was not just to wrap her liberally in warm, heat-retaining garments. We adopted a policy of choosing only the warmest days and of making frequent stops so that she could be out of her carrier to romp about and keep her circulation active. This brought a new dimension to the importance of warm weather. Regular rest periods reversed the situation. We were now apt to become inactive while Sarah was on the move.

If these ideas are kept in mind you can start them really young. Of course there are other problems that only experience can make truly obvious. Do you carry a layette? We chose to carry the basic materials for nappy changing in a packet suspended in the lower section of the papoose, much better than in the rucksack where food as well as extra clothing is stored. In the event we discovered that it was usually necessary to carry enough for only one nappy change since at this stage our walks were very short. Our aim was for baby to be kept happy in a convenient compromise with her parents' desires.

As soon as she was able to toddle about on her own feet we encouraged this. We never covered much ground but the young lady was enjoying herself, which mattered most, and before she had time to tire she was returned to the carrier to pull my hair for a while. This stop-go progress could be quite tiring for there was no chance to develop any rhythm. My wind was subjected to additional testing at this stage as I was often called upon to sing nursery rhymes in duet. "The Grand Old Duke of York" and "Jack and Jill" now have a personal significance that few nursery teachers will understand, and the breaking point nearly arrived on an ascent of Barf in roasting sunshine direct from the Swan Hotel, as those who know the route will readily appreciate. I must have lost pounds in weight during that short climb but the child's interest was maintained. The keynote was variety, for all concerned, and that was the factor which governed our every move.

As soon as her feet were big enough we bought a pair of the smallest boots available. This was a great moment. Sarah really thought she had grown up when she could wear her own boots, just like mummy and daddy, and the extra warmth and ankle support was of genuine significance even at two years. Warm trousers, anorak, woolly jumpers and cagoule were just as important. In time she began to carry her own tiny pack. It contained only her sandwiches and drink plus, at her own insistence, her cagoule. We wondered at first if this was asking too much but as she would not be parted from it there could be no doubt that this was an acceptable, indeed an enjoyable, part of the game.

Equal in importance with satisfactory clothing and accessories is the provision of incentive. It is useless to expect a child of tender years to find pleasure in walking for its own sake. The child may look the part but its motives are altogether different from those of an adult. Our answer was to make a game of every outing. We would look for small rocks to scramble over and if one looked vaguely the right shape it became a temporary "rocking-horse" to sit astride. I have lost count of the times we have played "ride-a-cock-horse" on some small boulder, grasping at a shoot of grass which represented the reins.

We would identify every incipient track as a sheep trod and wander from one to another in good-humoured deviation. Cairns had their uses too. I know there is much criticism of tracks being over-cairned but there is nothing like the prospect of adding one more pebble to the pile for getting junior moving in the right direction. A series of flat stones could be used as stepping stones whether over water or dry land and we would make progress by balancing on these, holding hands where necessary in case of insecure footing. Trees and large boulders could be used as hiding places and we would take it in turns to go ahead and lie in wait of supposedly unsuspecting followers. Needless to say, all these devices would take us in the desired direction.

As Sarah grew older we began to foster a wider interest in the environment. This meant simple identification of trees, plants and birds, apart from animals on farms we passed. In this respect my wife came into her own because of her particular interest in wild flowers. We would talk of the weather, the landscape, buildings and titbits of local history. Anything of interest would help to expand general knowledge and vocabulary, and it was never wasted. I never cease to be amazed about how retentive a young mind can be. In Grizedale Forest I pointed out a carpet of rich green leaves amongst the trees. "Look Sarah," I began, then looked to see if I had her attention. The pause was brief—but quite long enough. I had no time to continue. "It's wood sorrel, Daddy!" Her look expressed astonishment that I should show such ignorance. I glanced at my wife, whose eyes twinkled in amusement and I walked on in chastened silence. Sarah was then four years old and several months had passed since we had identified and discussed the plant, which had then been in flower.

By this time Sarah was climbing many of the smaller hills under her own steam. Before she was three she had reached the top of Sale Fell and walked the whole way on her own tiny feet with no word of complaint. Our simple route involved only 500 feet of ascent and she enjoyed every moment of it. Now aged seven—as I write—she seems to regard walking, and in particular climbing the hills, as an essential part of our leisure activities. To be on the safe side we always give her the choice between walking or some other pastime, which has meant that on some occasions we have visited shows, parks or playgrounds when we would much rather have been pulling on our boots to face the challenge of the hills. But you don't engender an interest in anything by making it compulsory. An evidence of our success has been seen in the occasions when Sarah has displayed genuine disappointment on learning that daddy has planned to go walking without her, even though it has been explained that the walk was far beyond her own modest capabilities.

There have been times when our jaunts have not given us the pleasure we would have enjoyed on our own. Usually this has been because progress was pathetically slow. Often her constant chatter has become an excruciating background to the proceedings, for she is an inveterate chatterbox and much too young to understand that dad can enjoy walking in silence, to appreciate the countryside for itself. Any wildlife must hear our approach from afar.

On the credit side are many moments of joy when she has shown a real pleasure in our surroundings. I remember an interval of incredible silence beside a tarn, followed by, "Look at that water sparkling!" This when a gentle breeze raised ripples that glistened like a dish of diamonds in the sun. There was a time when she spotted a baby red squirrel struggling in a steep bank of bracken at the roadside, and watched happily as we placed it safely back among the trees, away from passing cars and unsympathetic children playing on the shore of Loweswater nearby. Our only problem now appears to be the maintenance of personal fitness. The time is fast approaching when Sarah will outpace the pair of us!

3

FAMILY PLAYGROUNDS
(Wansfell Pike; Angletarn Pikes; Loughrigg; Catbells)

Some little hills take upon themselves the role of the family playground more readily than most. It is not simply a question of accessibility or ease of ascent, though these considerations are significant when very young children are taken to the hills, but the question of intrinsic interest is of paramount importance. No matter how easy a hill may be to climb, if it lacks attraction in outline or topography then the holiday crowds will be absent. How many folk do you see on the Mell Fells, Great and Little? You may not bother to go there yourself—which may help to prove the point—but if you do the answer is a foregone conclusion: not very many when compared with Catbells, for instance, and the reason is not just that Catbells is on the doorstep of tourist Keswick. It is a little hill with an immediate shapely appeal, it seems to hold no secrets from an inquisitive eye and it must be a prime contender for inclusion in this chapter.

Quite a number of little fells could justifiably find a place here but some have been rejected because they neatly fit into a different category and therefore find their niche elsewhere. Just three more hills complete this selection, each chosen for quite different qualities. Loughrigg is the sort of adventure playground of which city children can only dream and Wansfell Pike, right on the doorstep of Ambleside, provides a simple walk to a splendid viewpoint that makes it an ideal stroll for the first evening in the district. Angletarn Pikes is chosen mainly for its tarn. Perhaps Angletarn Pikes does not attract family parties in the same number as the other three but it certainly deserves this kind of attention. It has many of the qualities of the higher fells, and is quite the highest of this quartet, but I have no hesitation in including it as a representative of the family playgrounds.

WANSFELL PIKE

The popular stroll to Stock Ghyll Force is an Ambleside "must": along a winding way in a sylvan grotto with little side paths to viewpoints poised above the ravine's edge, over the bridge at the top where a brief detour to the hanging island gives careful visitors the thrill of a peep from above, and a descent of the true right bank to re-cross the beck and return to Ambleside. That is the way we always do it for the habit dies hard. It is only a brief stretch of the legs but delightful all the way, a short evening stroll of infinite charm.

Stock Ghyll is Wansfell's best-known stream, if only because of the waterfall. As a tourist hill Wansfell owes much to the patronage of Ambleside-based walkers. Although the ascent from Troutbeck is simple enough I suppose by far the majority of its climbers make their way to the summit by way of Stock Ghyll and up the western flank with its surprisingly steep final pull to the top. When they get there they can note with curiosity the adornment of an iron gate as they relax with the feeling of a job well done. But really they have not climbed Wansfell at all. This is Wansfell Pike. The true summit of the fell—the highest point—lies almost a mile to the north-east. It is labelled Baystones on the O.S. map, but it is debatable whether the extra effort of reaching it is worthwhile. It is indeed higher by some sixteen feet, but a foreground of grassy hummocks is no substitute for the magnificent view over Windermere provided by Wansfell Pike.

Perhaps the best place for looking at the fell is from a boat somewhere along the upper reach of Windermere. There is much to be said for the boatman's approach to a mountain region and one of the best ways into the Lake District is to enjoy a leisurely cruise on England's largest lake. That's the way we did it in the early days as Youth Hostel members, by train to Windermere station, then a wander down to the Bowness boat landings to board whichever of the British Rail's quartet of boats was next due on the cruise to Waterhead. Gentle tree-clad slopes, backed to the north and west by Lakeland's mountains, give added zest to your anticipations whether it be a first visit or a return. Wansfell Pike has its fair share of trees. They decorate the lower slopes, where Jenkin Crag is an often sought viewpoint, and provide a pleasant setting for afternoon or evening strolls with the family.

The woodland hereabouts is Skelghyll Wood. Walking here you are close to one of the district's busiest thorough-fares, the A591, but the cloak of trees muffles the sound of traffic. If you climb beyond the trees you will be standing above another route that links the Lake District with industrial northern England, though this link is hidden from view. The Thirlmere/Manchester aqueduct crosses Wansfell somewhere between the 700- and 800-foot con-tours. A stone column and a couple of old observatory towers help to locate it, if you can find them. An easier guide to its position is a series of iron gates, provided to smooth the way of the inspector whose job it is to make a periodic patrol of the pipeline to check for leakages. Lake-land's water is too precious to waste.

This area of fellside forms the base of Wansfell's south-west ridge, if ridge is not too extravagant a word to use in reference to what is in truth a rather undistinguished stretch of ground. It does have the appearance of a ridge, however, if you wander along the by-road from Low Wood to Troutbeck. Stop in the region of Holbeck Ghyll and look north. In the right conditions the skyline presents a dramatic enough silhouette. We once paused there to see the early sunshine illuminating the crest, so that the outline was sharp and clear in the moist morning air. With a few wisps of mist draping the lower slopes and veiling the soft greenery, with no high competitors to spoil the illusion, the crinkled crest had a commanding presence that brought the Cuillins of Skye momentarily to mind.

Alas, the reality could not be further from the jagged arêtes of those famous mountains of the Inner Hebrides. It is an exciting prospect but if you set out to climb it you will be sadly disappointed. Those craggy turrets turn out to be nothing more than brief rocky knolls on a slope of indefinite, tussocky ground, and the going is by no means easy. The position of Wansfell's Pike enjoys a mysterious uncertainty, in fact far back beyond the skyline, and not the least of problems is to select a route that avoids a maze of substantial, businesslike walls. As a line of ascent it is not particularly rewarding. The effort would be much better spent on a bigger fell—but do take the trouble to explore the lower, wooded slopes. That is where the interest lies.

A peculiarity of this small portion of Lakeland is the popularity of the spelling "ghyll". Purists would point out that this is an affectation. "Gill" is correct, maybe, but a glance at the map will show Holbeck Ghyll, Skelghyll and Stock Ghyll apart from features whose names are derived from such sources. In Langdale, not so far away, is the most famous poetic ghyll of all—Dungeon Ghyll—but the general rule is for the simpler version to be accepted. It is a good old north country word, but whatever the spelling it sounds the same.

You are not likely to meet many strangers on this side of Wansfell Pike. There is but one royal road to the summit, the way by Stock Ghyll with its family groups led by energetic small boys whose perspiring parents have promised them a hill climb—and if the day is warm have begun to regret the undertaking as they loiter in the wake of their active offspring. But they are inevitably drawn on and when they reach the top perhaps they find sufficient reward in the panorama.

Pride of place must go to Windermere's display with its armada of pleasure craft, each avoiding direct confrontation in spite of apparently casual navigation. At the far side of the lake the shining pool of Blelham Tarn is seen to advantage. The view north-west of Ambleside and the Rothay valley also holds great charm. I remember it late one autumn afternoon when we snatched an hour or so to walk on Wansfell as a break in our journey out of the district. After a day which had been for the most part wet, an eternity of steady drizzle that seemed to fill every nook and cranny of fell and valley, there came a break in the clouds and gentle sunshine raised a tenuous mist from the wooded countryside. Columns of smoke curled from a hundred chimneys to enhance a scene of lazy tranquillity and Ambleside rose from steaming trees like a lost city in a forgotten civilization.

But Wansfell is not always a place for peaceful meditation. In 1953 the calm of a hot June afternoon was shattered by a storm almost unrivalled in Ambleside's memory. In the town almost two and a half inches of rain were recorded in about three hours but the deluge that Wansfell suffered, particularly on the Troutbeck side where the storm centre seems to have been located, must have been much worse. Flood torrents resculpted sections of the fellside, trees and boulders were torn from the ground, walls and even roads were brushed aside. This sort of cloudburst is not unique. There have been much worse storms in the Lakeland hills but it is not so often that such displays of savage natural fury occur so close to centres of population. The areas of highest rainfall tend to keep company with the highest ground for, as every schoolchild knows from geography lessons, precipitation usually results from moist air rising over the mountains, but when these exceptional deluges come close to us we are made to realize how helpless mankind would be, but for a usually benign environment.

The paths of Wansfell have known tragedy too. Accidents and fatalities in the hills are usually associated with high mountains and crags, far from the reassuring aid of fortunately willing helpers. But mountains, large or small, have no compassion. The mortal remains of one walker lay undiscovered on modest Wansfell long after searchers had come to the conclusion that he could not be on the fell at all, but eventually his body was found not very far from a beaten track by a dog rooting in the bracken. The lesson is clear. Take care on all these little hills for their lack of stature is no guarantee of security.

Yet in spite of these moments of melodrama I like to remember Wansfell as a happy hill, ideal for the short family excursion, but equally rewarding if you have the odd hour to spare. You may choose it as a brief introduction to the district's fells or as a place for a spot of moderate exercise on an off-day. Whatever your reason for going there, Wansfell will provide a generous return for your modest efforts.

ANGLETARN PIKES

I suspect that Angle Tarn is a greater magnet than the fell that takes its name, especially when the sun shines warm and welcome as we expect on the best of summer days. Many pairs of boots must have been shed by its shore for hot toes to reap the benefit of its cooling, soothing waters and many family groups must have trudged up there with no more ambition than a happy afternoon beside the tarn.

This is one of the finest high-level tarns in the district. It is not a corrie tarn backed by dark vertical rock, rather a ridge tarn with some 400 yards of water cradled in a shallow bowl where all is light in a situation open to the sky. The land rises barely 250 feet to summits both north and south, for Angletarn Pikes has a junior partner in Brock Crags. Together they take this gem of a mountain lake under their wings to give token protection from the Cumbrian weather.

Much of the attraction of Angle Tarn stems from an indented shoreline and two rocky islets. Tiny bays contain pebbly beaches, miniature crags like models of the real thing plunge apologetically into the water and, in contrast, the reedy southern tip adds a completely different character to the scene. Here is no similarity with the better-known Angle Tarn of Langdale. Maybe the difference is one factor that makes this such a charming place for one who knows both tarns. Certainly it ranks among my best half-dozen of Lakeland tarns.

The ascent of Angletarn Pikes is one of the most obvious easy climbs available from Patterdale and judging by the well-trodden track it is a popular ascent too, though often it is only the first stage in the high-level route from Patterdale to the High Street range. Also worthy of consideration is an ascent over Brock Crags from the village of Hartsop. This route needs careful study on the map beforehand but once underfoot you can almost guarantee

solitude. One August we set out this way on a hot afternoon when the sun had brought a fair quantity of foot
traffic into the Hayeswater glen. Away from the valley we
hardly saw a soul until we reached Angle Tarn though
Hayeswater Gill was a veritable playground and the beck
an irresistible attraction for children whose parents pick-
nicked on nearby banks.

The lonely top of Brock Crags in some respects scores
over the main summit at Angletarn Pikes. This view of the
Hartsop valley is startling. Flat green pastures are scattered around like the fields of Arcadia and the glens of
upper Patterdale are laid out between the fingers of the
local fells. Brotherswater is the focal point in an attrac-
tively composed canvas, for this is one of the finest stations
for viewing the little lake. Formerly known as Broad-
water, it was renamed after a tragic accident in which two
brothers died in a skating accident.

Angletarn Pikes rivals Brock Crags in the excellence of
its valley panorama. There are two summits. The higher
top gives a view of Ullswater, Brotherswater is again well
seen and the sudden deep drop to Patterdale emphasizes
the steep slopes of these hills. This top might have been
specially constructed for looking into Deepdale, across the
main strath. You seem to be perched in the upper balcony
of some stupendous theatre, a "seat in the gods" as we
used to call it. Even better is the view from the Boardale
Hause/Angle Tarn track, just below. For a quarter of a
mile this is a traverse in space. A plunging fellside sweeps
with no interruption down to the intake walls, giving the
impression that it could not be any steeper without exposing the bedrock of the fell. The abrupt slope is framed by
rocks. Dubhow Crag and Fall Crag are tall pillars which
form borders for the dizzy view.

Angletarn Pikes cannot compete in altitude with the
great mountains of Cumbria and with the valley floor
already some 500 feet above sea-level the ascent can
hardly be described as a taxing undertaking. Still, two
rocky peaks, splendid views and the promise of water for
bathing can make it a climb to remember long after the
summer months have gone. It is a grand little hill where

young and old can enjoy a taste of mountain adventure, and that jewel of a tarn places it in a class of its own.

LOUGHRIGG

Many of Cumbria's famous mountains, commanding of aspect and distinguished in altitude, would be put to shame if set within Loughrigg's geographical boundaries. The fell may not be very high, just over a thousand feet, but it covers an extensive—and devious—stretch of terrain. Circumnavigate its margins and you will have completed a walk of eight miles, or thereabouts, eight miles enclosing the best part of three square miles of Lakeland in miniature. The many diminutive streams, valleys, tarns, crags and summits in a setting of woodland and lakes form a Lilliputian mountain system which is a perfect introduction to the fells for any newcomer who has ideas of taking up fell walking. In essence, the character of the district as a whole is to be found in this relatively small area.

Loughrigg Fell is the correct name. A glance at the map will confirm this but no one ever uses the full title. Loughrigg means "Lakes Ridge", which is apt enough. Apart from its own namesake tarn there are many smaller pools which have their places in various hollows about the fell. A favourite of mine is Lily Tarn with its minikin islet, a place of pleasant memories open to the sky which always seems to diffuse an aura of light and happiness. Most walks on Loughrigg seem to bring us to Lily Tarn eventually and we always like to linger by its grassy shores and enjoy the sunshine by its rippling surface—and always there is sunshine. There is no magic about the Loughrigg weather, of course. The fell is just as much prone to the vagaries of the Lake District climate as any other, but the sun is so important a constituent of the pleasures of Loughrigg that we would never dream of going there in any but the best conditions. To wander round a corner and see the sun lighting the surface of some unsuspected pool is one of the delights of the place. Loughrigg has more than its fair share of lakes too, for Grasmere, Rydal Water, Elterwater and Windermere help to mark its limits. You would be hard put to find a spot on the fell that is out of the sight of water.

The Grasmere flank boasts the most populous path on the fell, Loughrigg Terrace, beloved by many a gentle walker who would never otherwise dream of stepping away from the paved way. It is a fine short walk with a superb outlook over Grasmere's sweet vale, but it is no introduction to the veritable maze of tracks beyond. This multiplicity of tracks is another of the joys of Loughrigg but they can be a real trap for the unwary. They wend their way round sundry hillocks, along tiny valleys, beside walls and to the very edge of crags. In mist it must be a tortuous labyrinth and even on a clear day it can be puzzling enough—like Snakes and Ladders played for real. One sunny afternoon we came across a poor soul completely lost near Lily Tarn, despite having the appropriate Wainwright guide in his grasp. He had to be directed to Ambleside, less than half a mile distant.

The summit is distinguished by an O.S. column, though two nearby tops cannot be far short of it in height. Scattered about the fell are numerous subsidiary summits, many of them cairned. Four in particular have excellent views. From Todd Crag and Ivy Crag the prospect of Windermere is outstanding and an unnamed eminence between Ivy Crag and the summit provides the viewpoint *par excellence* for Loughrigg Tarn. The Grasmere Cairn's name speaks for itself.

Screened by trees on the slope above Rydal Water is a surprise in the shape of a huge cave, the result of quarrying operations in the past. Unlike the majority of man-made holes in the Lake District this one is safe to penetrate and is big enough to provide shelter for all the walkers on the fell should they be caught in a sudden downpour—and that includes any water-logged refugees from the over-populated highway of Loughrigg Terrace, just half a mile away. A large deep pool in the entrance is home for shoals of tiny fish and, in season, for a huge population of tadpoles. An exciting place for children, this, but watch them on the path across the top of the cave. To look down is simple, but a fall is easily accomplished too and the deep end of the pool is a difficult target—assuming they can swim! This track is best avoided by over-adventurous youngsters.

My latest visit to Loughrigg was a pre-breakfast stroll that became a trot when lazy progress put the bacon and eggs at risk. In some dozen visits it was the first time I have walked truly alone, but later in the day the fell was itself again. When I looked from the Grasmere road the tracks were busy with folk enjoying an Indian summer on a fine October afternoon. But at eight o'clock the wind had had an edge to it, enough to remind me that winter was just around the corner.

Loughrigg makes a diverting change from the legion of long and strenuous walks which many of us too often make our staple diet. A day of wandering on this modest fell is a day well spent and when you eventually reach the top on one of those sunny days that allow you to settle down for a spell of quiet contemplation, the southern and eastern summits are ideal havens from the throngs of light-hearted holiday-makers at 1,101 feet. You can take your ease and watch the school parties come and go, see the cheerful family groups enjoy their moments of triumph, note the young in heart as they step spryly up to the O.S. column and the young in fact race to be the first to balance on its ultimate inches. Loughrigg is truly a happy fell and you will feel that nothing much can be wrong with the world when so many can so obviously enjoy these un-sophisticated pleasures of our natural heritage. It is the sort of place that seems to crave these attentions, with its intricate puzzles seemingly laid out to be solved in party mood. Walking on Loughrigg is not fell walking on the grand scale, but it often seems so and is never dull. This little fell is generous in its rewards—if you have not done so already, try it soon.

CATBELLS

Small boys see Catbells and straight away feel the urge to take up mountaineering—and their grandparents are still content if they can tackle the hill when the bigger fells make demands they can no longer meet. Parties of school children spending a week with the Holiday Fellowship in the hostel at Stair often make for Catbells on their first day out. Youth Hostellers from Keswick look across Derwentwater and feel that it is the ideal appetizer at the beginning of a week on the fells. Catbells may be only a hill, and quite a small one at that, but it has the shape of a mountain, a shape that attracts the attention of anyone with a feeling for high places—but especially it is a hill for the young.

Perhaps the attraction of Catbells to children is in part due to the name. Surely no writer of children's stories could invent one better. We are told that it is derived from "cat bields", suggesting that it once held shelter for the wildcat and that may well be so, but the very sound of it holds a breath of enchantment. For my own daughter it really is a fairytale mountain. From very early days she delighted in the make-believe world of the tales of Beatrix Potter and for Sarah this has always been "Mrs Tiggy-winkle's Mountain". As soon as she was able we traced the path of young Lucie from Little Town to the prickly washerwoman's home on the fell, and all the time she chattered away as though she had been there before.

One of the delights of Catbells is its position. As the final upthrust of a splendid ridge, one of the finest in Lakeland, it manages to convey an impression of isolation with the col of Hause Gate clearly separating it from neighbouring Maiden Moor. The summit projects a sensation of airy independence so often absent on higher hills where the build-up on most sides may eliminate much of the depth from the view. Except to the south the top is surrounded by space, a downward sweep of a thousand feet or more. This study in depth offers a prospect of great variety.

To the east is the island-speckled waterscape of Derwentwater looking for all the world like a boating pool in a park, with a fleet of toy-town vessels weaving a pattern of wakes upon the summer-time waters. South of the lake is Grange and its sylvan surroundings, a brief preview of the land of promise beyond the Jaws of Borrowdale. Turn about and see the green fields of Newlands where pastoral tranquillity is the key to one of the most placidly beautiful of valleys. There is no substantial village to be seen and even the few cottages of Stair try to hide among trees. The mouth of the valley is closed by the mysterious little hill of Swinside, resting like a football on the penalty spot, waiting for the boot of Catbells to shoot it through the goalmouth formed by Grisedale Pike and Skiddaw. It leads the eye over Bassenthwaite Lake to the wide coastal plain on the fringe of the Solway Firth.

This is truly a panorama in which valleys hold the stage. The backcloth of mountains merely helps to focus the eye on the lowland scene, but if you trouble to look to the hills you see them as they really are. There is none of the foreshortening inevitable in valley views, yet you are still below the tops of the encircling fells so that they do not suffer in apparent stature when compared with your viewpoint. Proportion is everything in a view and here on Catbells the views come close to perfection.

Catbells may be a playground today but it was a working fell before it reached the age of retirement. There are old mines on both sides of the hill, at Yewthwaite, Brandelhow and elsewhere. They are all long closed but spoil heaps, shafts and levels still abound though the most dangerous holes have been made safe. Somehow the workings do not intrude overmuch. Nature and time are healers and a covering of mosses and grass has softened the harsher outlines of the scars.

A contribution to the Catbells scene along the eastern margin is the trees. One of the delights of Derwentwater is its attendant woodlands which, viewed from a boat, seem to come down to the water's edge on all sides. This is a lake where the trees seem to grow out of the water itself. The woods of Manesty, Brandelhow and Hawse End cloak the attempt of Catbells to dip its toes in the lake. The paths through the trees are fairy grottos, an impression heightened by the chorus of birdsong and the sparkle of water glimpsed occasionally between the leaves. Red squirrels are holding their ground too. We found one rooting in a discarded lunch pack at Hawse End and it scampered reluctantly away into the trees only at the very last moment.

Catbells is essentially a fair-weather fell. For me it is a hill for a morning stroll so that the exquisite views can be enjoyed before being blurred by the hazy heat of a warm summer day. I remember one morning when we set out from Stair in pleasant sunshine, ambling unhurriedly along the road to Skelgill. We reached the top from Hause Gate before the crowds arrived and a cool breeze made an extra jumper necessary as we stood and gazed around. Newlands looked particularly good that morning with the green patchwork of fields an even richer hue than usual following recent rain, and the ridges across the valley stood clear and sharp in the moist air. Causey Pike, surely seen at its best from here, hurled across a superb challenge. Further to the left the ridge of Hindscarth looked as good as ever and Robinson appeared as a mountain giant. A skyline of peaks jostled for attention but we put them all out of mind. It was simply sufficient to stand on little Catbells and enjoy rewards quite out of proportion to the modest effort required for its ascent. Once again I reflected that this is a fell for all ages and above all a fell for the family.

4

FELLS OF THE NORTHERN FRINGE
(A Lonely Land Back o' Skidda')

Even a casual visitor to Keswick who does not hear of
Skiddaw must be a very rare creature indeed and I should
imagine that the average fell walker is not long in getting
Keswick's venerable guardian beneath his boots, as well
as the neighbouring Blencathra for that matter. However,
these two fells and their intermediate satellites make
an effective mountain curtain to hide the shy northern
fells beyond, a curtain parted only slightly where the
Glenderaterra Beck carves a steeply flanked valley to
escape the clutches of the Caldew basin. Motorists travelling north to Keswick can catch a glimpse of the usually
hidden hills "Back o' Skidda'" from various points along
the road from Dunmail Raise. Great Calva and the gentle
skyline of Knott peer like a couple of curious kittens
through the unexpected gap, but all else is hidden. The
northern group is only revealed to folk who travel the
by-ways to Calbeck, maybe prompted by an interest in the
song extolling the deeds of the local folk-hero, John Peel,
or to those who climb the popular pair of hills just to the
south.

This neglect should occasion little surprise. Inevitably
attention must turn to the exciting hills of central and
southern Lakeland where stimulating and well-publicized
outlines beckon boldly. But there are other hills, quietly
waiting in the north, and though they lack the Romantic
thrills of the Scafells and their companions it would be a
shame to discard them unseen and untried. That the majority of walkers ignore these outliers is perhaps no bad
thing in these crowded days for even at the peak of the
holiday season you can find solitude in this lonely backwater.

The highest point in the group is the 2,329-foot summit of Knott in the middle of an extensive flat top, a smooth and generally featureless expanse of grass. This is a characteristic shared by the majority of its neighbours, a factor which emphasizes the main difficulty encountered in walking hereabouts. It is important to be able to navigate accurately with map and compass for if mist closes down you can soon be in trouble in a place where one grassy slope looks much like another. I remember a trip made in thick mist from High Pike to Great Calva by way of Knott. All was plain sailing as far as the bothy on Great Lingy Hill, for a wide, well-marked track serves the hut and the nearby sheep pens, but thereafter lies a featureless region some three miles across as the walker strides.

A walk without views could have been cause for disappointment but, in fact, the mist made the day. Here was an opportunity to try route-finding skills in blind conditions over what was then unknown territory. With compass in hand I progressed from one grassy tussock to another, each time locking my eyes on to a tuft at the verge of visibility. It was a great feeling to locate the few stones which pass for a summit cairn on Knott and even better to find at first attempt the col leading to Great Calva. All that was to be seen between the hut on Great Lingy Hill and the fence on Great Calva were the few square feet of turf around me and that tiny cairn on Knott. Probably I was lucky. I once found it even easier to get lost in similar conditions on a fell which I supposed I knew. It was disconcerting on Wetherlam to set off in the direction of Swirl How and a few minutes later find myself approaching a top that I had thought was behind me. The fells have a knack of quickly bringing you to earth if you tend to get a bit above yourself!

The culminating feet of Great Calva have more to commend them than those of Knott for there are a few stones about the place and the top is easier to locate because it is traversed by a fence, a safe guide to the Caldew and Dash valleys. The rocks have been used in the construction of a couple of cairns, one at an angle in the fence, the other marking the summit a hundred yards or so further north.

A few yards east is one of the most effective wind shelters to be found on any fell. I have been able to light a pipe here in a major gale with the expenditure of a single match. Pipemen will recognize a rare and blissful moment.

Away to the east is the craggy bastion of Carrock Fell, the final outpost of the Lakeland fells in this north-eastern corner and a grand contrast to the smooth, slate-based hills found elsewhere on the northern fringe. The boulder-littered southern flank of this comparatively rough chunk of upland can be climbed direct from the Caldew valley and there is easy access from the north, but I prefer to approach from the east where there is opportunity to park a car alongside the unfenced road. The wall of rock facing the road consists, in part, of the same material as the Cuillin ridges of Skye, gabbro. It is the only place north of the A66 that can be of interest to the cragsman, though the routes are too short to command a great deal of attention. It is no obstacle to fell walkers, however. An obvious breach on the left leads quickly to the rim of the escarpment which is followed to its highest point, from where you head due west to the summit across half a mile of rising heather decorated with a sprinkling of boulders.

This summit is unique. It sports more rock than the rest of the tops in this chapter put together, and here is no haphazard scatter of rocks. This is the ruin of an ancient hill fort. The position of the encircling wall is clearly distinguishable as a mound of stones, continuous except for gaps at the four points of the compass which reasonable deduction suggests were gateways. The enclosed area measures some 250 by 100 yards. These ruins have suffered to produce a sheep fold and a large cairn on a tiny outcrop within the enclosure.

When I went up there in heavy rain I sat beside this cairn to enjoy a solitary lunch under the protection of the best, cheapest and most adaptable piece of foul-weather gear I have ever owned. This was a simple cape produced by the Pac-a-mac people. It folded into a small enough parcel to fit easily into a pocket and when in use it slipped over the head, covering my rucksack too, giving a splendidly effective defence against the heaviest rain. I have never had anything better for general walking. When I stopped for lunch it became a midget tent, if the weather was wet enough to make such protection desirable, since it was capacious enough for me to retire completely within its protective skin. Its only fault was its colour. In these safety-conscious days it is considered wise to be conspicuous, but my black cape tended to merge into the surroundings. On one occasion, after enjoying a dry after-lunch pipe in a typical downpour, I emerged from my cocoon with an eruption of smoke reminiscent of an infant volcano to gaze into the apprehensive eyes of a passing walker for whom this was obviously the first intimation of my presence. That cape has long since perished and its replacements have never matched the all-round utility of their predecessor.

Carrock Fell's rock ends at the summit. The wide western flank is a marshy tract of moorland that has little in common with the rest of the fell. Nor is there any real similarity with the hills over on the western edge of this group where there are five tops conveniently known as the Uldale Fells. These spring from the north ridge of Knott, with two subsidiary ridges leading west. The highest point in this western group is a Great Sca Fell, where a tiny cairn set in the midst of a grassy veldt seems to emphasize the contrast between this gentle mound and the savage might of its illustrious namesake. Further north the ridge bifurcates and the recess of Charleton Gill separates Brae Fell from Longlands Fell. The small cairn on the latter is put to shame by the splendid affair on the former. Neither fell presents problems in ascent. The west ridge of Great Sca Fell has two tops. Meal Fell, the nearer, has a summit marked by a shallow circular windshelter of only token efficiency. The strangely named Great Cockup had no cairn at all on my visit.

The most adequate reason for allowing the last two fells their separate identities is the dramatic nature of their separation. The smooth progression of the ridge is unexpectedly interrupted by an abrupt cutting, a groove exposing minor, slaty crags on either side. Compared with the great declivities around Wasdale Head it is a mere scratch, but in the context of the Uldale Fells this is an incident of more than passing consequence. Trusmadoor is well worth a visit. It seems likely that its origins date from the last ice age for it has all the marks of a glacial overflow channel, eroded by melt waters pent in Burntod Gill by an accumulation of ice in the Dash valley. Trusmadoor irresistibly brings to mind a picture in a book I owned as a child. Moses stood imperiously on the shore of the Red Sea, his staff held in horizontal command over waters which were parted to allow the Israelites to pass with impunity through an enormous V-shaped cleft.

Sheep have their personal heaven in this land of grass and freedom. I once took lunch by Trusmadoor and watched countless hordes of the woolly creatures graze on the flanks of Burn Tod across the valley. I remember thinking that if you were to attempt a midnight count of such a legion as an aid to sleep the net result would probably be nightmare. A peaceful silence was broken when a solitary sheep gave voice to her satisfaction in the ample provender, her song of praise being taken up on all sides until a ripple of bleating spread across the fellside in an echoing chorus of joy. The cantata faded into silence, a lull which lasted some moments before the whole sequence was repeated. There followed encore upon encore. As I sat listening as an audience of one I felt a sudden sense of the comic in the process and burst out laughing. It seemed so outrageously funny.

Of all these northern fells perhaps the finest individual is High Pike. A hill which boasts so splendid a name might be expected to dominate its surroundings like the popular conception of a true mountain. When a study of a geological map shows that it coincides with a zone of rock bearing the illustrious name of the Borrowdale Volcanic Series then the fell walker's imagination is fired with curiosity. However, those who hurry round to Caldbeck with hopes of finding a little bit of Borrowdale outside its natural setting are due for disappointment. When they get there they may need to glance at their map if High Pike is to be identified with certainty.

Yet despite such an inauspicious prelude the journey

will not have been in vain. Though this is not a pike to
rival its Langdale brethren it is still the high point of an
area of interesting country, gentle in comparison with
Pike o' Stickle and Harrison Stickle maybe, but those who
take the trouble to explore will realize that their efforts
have been worthwhile.

High Pike is clearly separated from the rest of this
northern group by the valleys of Carrock Beck to the east
and Dale Beck in the west. The latter stream belongs to
the village of Caldbeck. After a change of names which
turns it into Parkend Beck it passes through the little
settlement to join the River Caldew—as Carrock Beck has
done some three miles up-river. Much of the land enclosed
by these watercourses is pastoral in character so that,
though High Pike may seem vast according to such techni-
cal limits the actual area of open fell is far smaller.

Dale Beck is the more fascinating of these boundary
streams. Quite unknown to almost all of Lakeland's transient visitors, this is a beck of outstanding interest. It
starts life on the marshy uplands of Knott, south-west of
High Pike's summit, but soon enters an exciting phase of
its existence where the grandeur of central Lakeland
really is called to mind. This is Roughton Gill, a rocky
ravine in the best tradition, abounding in plunging
cascades and full of the sound of tumbling water. It com-
pares favourably with many of the tourist attractions that
pull in the crowds elsewhere in the district.

Roughton Gill was the scene of extensive mining activity in days gone by—so was Carrock Beck for that
matter—but the miners have long since gone, leaving
little but an obscure history behind. I suppose most folk
have heard of Coppermines Valley at Coniston or the
Greenside Mines under Helvellyn but the evidences of
industry are too obvious to miss in the shadow of the
popular fells. In this sequestered valley the industrial
remains are easily found but the scars have been softened
by the passage of time much more effectively, and in any
case large-scale mining is less recent, so they hardly intrude on the landscape in quite so devastating a way. Some
of the caves add interest to their surroundings and some

The western slopes of the Howgill Fells

Track into the Howgill Fells from the north near Gaisgill

View southwards from the path near Angle Tarn with Caudale Moor and Red Screes in the background

Angletarn Pikes cast their reflection on the still surface of Brotherswater

The cave above Rydal on Loughrigg Fell

Family party on a Loughrigg footpath

Looking over Derwentwater to Lonscale Fell and Blencathra, from the terraced track below Catbells

Longlands Fell on the north-western edge of the Uldale Fells

Whitewater Dash north of Skiddaw

Dale Beck in the Caldbeck Fells

The ridge of Knott Rigg with High Stile and Red Pike in the background

Kentmere Church with Kentmere Hall to the left. The slopes of
Sallows are shadowed; the Garburn Pass goes over the saddle
above the Hall

Winter at Grasmere. A patch of sunlight rests upon Seat Sandal

Loweswater on the extreme right and Carling Knott and Burnbank
Fell which rise from its wooded southern shore

The wintry summit of Ullock Pike

walkers are happy to seek them out as curiosities that bring a touch of variety to a day in the hills.

The Roughton Gill mines were among the first to be established in the Lake District, long before the birth of tourism, dating back to Elizabethan times when lead and copper were extracted in commercial quantities. More than a score of minerals have been found here, indeed the place is a happy hunting ground for amateur geologists who can usually be found pottering about on the old spoil heaps. Although the hinterland may be largely unvisited, Roughton Gill is likely to have a sprinkling of preoccupied individuals assiduously picking over the rubble. On a sunny weekend you can walk by to the accompaniment of apparently random tapping from hammers playing tuneful compositions for percussion, a sound peculiar to this productive spot.

Roughton Gill splashes on with gay abandon into a deeply carved dale where, as Dale Beck, it wends a less hurried way along a level strath with many a grassy sward offering its invitation to picknickers—if they can trouble themselves to wander the short distance from their cars. More usually the folding chairs are opened a few yards from the roadside, as a tour of the Calbeck by-ways will prove. Yet the exploration of this sheltered bowl in the hills, with its meandering beck, is an attractive proposition on a warm summer afternoon.

However, it is after leaving the protective arms of the fells that Dale Beck undergoes its most startling metamorphosis. Now renamed Park Beck it suddenly enters a narrow region of carboniferous limestone and just before entering Caldbeck it takes a joyful tumble and dons the characteristics of a true limestone stream. Here is the Howk, a short but deep ravine. Overhung by greenery and echoing to the surge of excited water, it is more than reminiscent of similar formations in the Craven District of Yorkshire.

The whole scene is quite different from anything else in the National Park. There are swallow holes and caves, natural ones for a change—the Old Man of the mines played no part in the development of this little sideshow—and the length of the gorge can be traced along a carefully constructed path. The approach along a sylvan glade is entirely charming and even the ruins of Caldbeck's bobbin mill do not seem out of place in this shady glen.

I have talked with people who claim to know Lakeland but have never heard of the Howk. They may have been to Caldbeck even, but John Peel's grave seems to be the attraction. They go away without knowing what they are missing and they are the losers. If they like to walk the fells they may turn to High Pike for a little exercise, but no one can really claim to know High Pike who has not made himself familiar with Dale Beck in all its guises, with its transition from slaty upland, through volcanic rocks to limestone. It is a lesson in geology set out to be read page by page, like a book in three chapters, but no book ever written has ever described the science of geology in quite as entertaining a fashion as Dale Beck.

Yet there is much more to High Pike than any of its boundary streams may suggest. Men have sought and taken mineral wealth from beneath the grassy acres for many a century and Roughton Gill has not had a monopoly in their endeavour. Carrock Beck, too, has seen its share in their activities. Driggeth Mine has shafts at nearly 2,000 feet above sea level and on the northern slopes of the fell are Potts Gill and Sandbed mines, closed now but operational until not so many years ago. The vicinity of these mines is riddled with old shafts. Generally they are fenced—the sheep need protection even if walkers are relatively rare—but not all the barriers are in first-rate condition, though the most dangerous of the pitfalls seem to be adequately protected.

One group of workings is of particular interest for an insight it gives into the ways of the old-time miner—the Old Man, or T'Owd Man is his historical folk-title, a name that rises from the misty realms of industrial folklore. Near the excellent track across the fell, the through route to the hut and sheep pens on Great Lingy Hill, there are groups of shafts dotted apparently at random over the northern slopes of High Pike. Above one dark entry you can see, if you take the trouble to look, a vein of mineral which is certainly the reason for this particular series of holes. The shafts are arranged in line, as are others on the fell, and some groups can be lined up with others even at a distance, illustrating the way in which useful deposits occupy faults in the prevailing rock. When these were near the surface the miners would find it convenient to sink shafts at close intervals rather than pursue an extended course underground.

There were mines all over these fells north of the A66, on Knott and Carrock Fell as well as on Blencathra and Bannerdale Crags. The whole area is rich in mining history. The saying, "Caldbeck Fells are worth all England else", has its origins in this mineral wealth. The old-timers had scant regard for scenic values but they did appreciate the profit motive, just as much as any modern financier.

Until the early 1950s much of High Pike was maintained as a grouse moor, in common with other open fell country at this side of the Caldew. Evidence of such sporting interest can be seen in the presence of shooting hides, or butts, now generally in a state of disrepair. The hut on Great Lingy Hill would have been used by sportsmen as a shelter. It is still a handy refuge for shepherds and wayfarers in general. In the early sixties the hut was a welcome haven from a violent squall after a crossing from Carrock Fell, and as the heavens opened I enjoyed relative comfort while the elements raged furiously outside. Lunch was accompanied by the rattle of hail upon robust wooden walls.

On a more recent family visit we found that a modest visitors' book is now provided, though it is treated with scant respect by some members of youthful parties. It would seem that walkers frequent the area more than was the case even a decade previously, although by comparison with central Lakeland these fells remain deserted. We saw only four people during a whole afternoon and two of those were at a distance.

It was a leisurely day. The weather at the foot of the fell was quite typical of what we had come to expect in an

extended season of splendid sunshine, but haze on high
masked the sun to some effect and conditions were surprisingly cool. A cold wind on the summit had us seeking out a
sheltered spot when the time came to open our lunch
packets.

It is three miles—as the curlew flies—from Caldbeck to
the summit of its patron fell. We drove to Nether Row and
almost halved that distance as a concession to Sarah's
tender years, but our route from there was so eccentric as
to more than cancel out any saving in mileage. This starting point is near the 1,000-foot contour, a consideration
when you have a toddler with you. With gentle gradients
and high access points, these northern fells must be the
easiest of all to climb, certainly among those in excess of
2,000 feet. After an initially zigzag course as we pottered
around inspecting the old mines, our final approach was
made in direct line. The slope is so undemanding that
there is no particular advantage in keeping to the marked
way, unless misty weather is in prospect. The ancient
cairn on Low Pike can be mistaken for the summit as you
make your way up this tussocky terrain, but it is little
more than an easing of the slope. Beyond it, only about 500
feet away, is the true top.

There is no mistaking the summit of High Pike. Though
the highest ground on the fell has little in the way of
natural adornment to distinguish it from the surrounding
acres, man has added his own decorations so that the place
is unique among the rolling northern hills. This is Caldbeck's beacon fell. The large, bare patch—occupied by fire
on really important occasions—has for company the ruins
of a shepherd's cottage. Both are situated at the limit of the
level summit ridge, commanding a view of the pleasantly
green vale of the Caldew—the northern reach where the
river has shaken off the shackles of the hills—and beyond
is the more open land of the Eden valley. To the north you
see the Solway Firth defending some of Scotland's gentler
hills.

Perhaps a hundred yards south of this viewpoint is an
ample heap of stones, some of which have been pilfered to
build a more orthodox cairn. No doubt the men of the

Ordnance Survey turned to this ready supply when they raised their own familiar construction nearby. As a proof of their latest attention my newest version of the one-inch Tourist Map credits the fell with an altitude of 2,159 feet, an increase of two feet on past issues.

High Pike's most distinctive unnatural feature stands beside these stony embellishments. It is an artifact upon which many a visitor must have happily reclined, a substantial seat set up as a memorial to a young man of Nether Row and, since 1970, to his mother. It seems a nice way to be remembered, to offer a restful interlude to those who also find peace and pleasure in wandering upon the lonely uplands "back o' Skidda'".

5

OFF THE BEATEN TRACK

(Ard Crags and Knott Rigg; Applethwaite Common; Seat Sandal; the Fells of Wythop)

Sometimes even the most gregarious of walkers feels the urge to get away from the throng. Despite complaints that the Lake District is becoming overcrowded there is no difficulty in finding room for a quiet walk, for though the popular fells may, on a Bank Holiday afternoon, resemble Blackpool's promenade you can—with a little imagination—find a spot where the chances are that you will have the hill to yourself. The fells are traditionally the grazing ground of sheep but there are times when you may look around and wonder if all those sheep really are four-legged. Stand near the top of Seat Sandal on an August Bank Holiday weekend, for instance, and look at the wide track to Helvellyn that zigzags up the southern flank of Dollywaggon Pike. You may stand alone as you watch walkers by the hundred plod a personal pilgrimage to the roof of Lakeland's genial giant—and how many of them bother to introduce a little variety to the route by making the detour along the rim of the escarpment to visit Dollywaggon Pike and Nethermost Pike? Not many, you may be sure, though it is a much more rewarding way. I recently walked a direct line from Seat Sandal to Dollywaggon Pike and as I crossed the Helvellyn Highway at right angles to the traffic flow groups of walkers gazed with apparent astonishment, their eyes seeming to recognize a lunatic at large, coming out of nowhere and to all intents and purposes heading nowhere.

Not so long ago we spent a full week on the fells, including August Bank Holiday weekend, and only once did we meet a fellow walker on a summit. We saw few others elsewhere during our walks. These were moderate hills, for young Sarah was with us, but they gave us quite as much pleasure as any of the fells where we knew the crowds would be congregating. Not one of them is included in this chapter, but they and many more are free for anyone to enjoy. The examples described in the following pages may not be quite the loneliest fells in Lakeland but their tracks will never resemble the scars on Helvellyn. With a map and a little initiative anyone can find a private and personal paradise off the beaten track.

ARD CRAGS AND KNOTT RIGG

A favourite perch of mine is on the ridge running south-west from Eel Crag towards Whiteless Pike and Buttermere. Where this escarpment rises to the undistinguished summit of Wandope and the edge falls away sharply to the valley of Sail Beck, I like to sit with my open lunch packet and enjoy a breathtaking prospect of ridges stretching range after range across the landscape like a series of breakers curling towards a distant seashore. Seven ridges I have counted, culminating in the long line of the Helvellyn Dods, some quite small in stature but each perfectly proportioned so that this is a view of mountains in an undoubted mountain region.

The nearest ridge is formed by Ard Crags and Knott Rigg. Though within easy reach of some of Lakeland's most popular centres—Keswick is only four miles away and Buttermere is even nearer—these two fells are among the quietest in the district. One lovely summer afternoon, the first Monday in August, we went up there with every likelihood of enjoying a peaceful walk. We were not disappointed. Across the valley of Rigg Beck a steady procession followed the skyline between Causey Pike and Eel Crag. The track in the valley had its visitors too and hardly more than a mile away traffic cluttered the tarmac strip on Newlands Hause, yet Ard Crags was ours to enjoy without disturbance.

These are slate-based fells and show the common characteristics of such country. The ridge is smooth, clothed in grass on Knott Rigg but giving way to heather along the crest of Ard Crags. On either side are steep slopes. It is on one of these slopes that Ard Crags's most intriguing feature is to be found. South of the summit and well up the fellside above the side valley of Ill Gill are the Keskadale Oaks, possibly a rare example of the indigenous tree cover of the district. Most trees growing in Lakeland today owe their existence to the hand of man. Many were planted by landowners anxious to improve their landscape but others have commercial origins, as exemplified by the modern example of the Forestry Commission. In the past coppice woods provided charcoal for smelting iron and making gunpowder, and the bobbin industry made good use of mature timber. Plastic is the thing nowadays. It is likely that the Keskadale Oaks were cut for industrial use since most of the trees have developed from shoots springing from old stumps. However, it is interesting to speculate that this could be a relict woodland and a link with prehistoric Cumbria. Could most of the fellsides have resembled this in ancient times?

Keskadale is a branch of the Newlands Valley and marks the south-eastern limit of both Ard Crags and Knott Rigg. The northern and western boundaries are defined by the deep troughs of Rigg Beck and Sail Beck so that there are connecting passes between Keswick and Buttermere on either side of the ridge; the latter for the walker and the Newlands route for the motorist. The ridge has its roots where these valleys meet in Newlands and rises to a distinct crest before falling to Newlands Hause. Beyond the road the ridge merges with the north-west shoulder of Robinson, of which it is really an elongated spur.

This relationship is not entirely obvious from a casual glance at the map. The road tends to dominate the picture but the reality is that Sail Beck forms the main lateral valley from Buttermere and the road leaves this to cross the watershed and enter Keskadale where Keskadale Beck flows east from a source high on the western flank of Robinson. If the Sail Beck pass was not 500 feet higher than Newlands Hause it is likely that the road would go that way. The famous hause would then be an unimportant and probably nameless depression and the ridge would come into its own as a splendid high-level approach to Robinson from Newlands. As it is the road is an effective barrier as far as fell walkers are concerned. Those who climb Robinson from this side tend to start from a car parked at the summit of the pass.

The easiest way on to our ridge is from the road at Newlands Hause. Not much more than 700 feet of gentle climbing brings the summit of Knott Rigg underfoot and the continuation to Ard Crags is even easier, but such tactics are a cheat. Honest walkers will tackle the delightful ridge from Rigg Beck and make a circular trip of it by returning down Keskadale Edge to the lonely house of Keskadale on the Newlands–Buttermere road. This combination gives a splendid route for a short summery afternoon.

When we took Sarah on these fells we found a rather more exciting variation, the lonely dell of Ill Gill below the Keskadale Oaks. The sparsity of tracks suggests that few walkers go this way, which is hardly surprising for the little valley becomes quite steep, making progress a minor achievement on a hot and sultry day such as we chose. In fact, with an active child on my back, little persuasion was needed when the suggestion came that we should take an early break for lunch. Out came the sandwiches and flasks, but our stay was unexpectedly short. Our grassy couch proved less uninhabited than we had thought and when several colonies of ants invited themselves to lunch an abrupt departure was precipitated.

The Keskadale Oaks are well in view at the entrance to the gill. The simple track at the outset soon deteriorates, but the accompanying stream of warbles a liquid refrain of encouragement and at one point water slithers down an exposed slab of rock on the left. Beyond the waterslide there is a sensation of mild pioneering in a miniature wilderness. The scenery is as good as anything of its kind in north-west Lakeland, considering the size of the ravine. Though the scale is small, the proportions are perfect.

The top of Knott Rigg is an excellent spot for a sunny afternoon but the high point, in every sense, is the little roof-top of Ard Crags. The view is restricted to the north and south by higher land, but less so than from Knott Rigg which retires further into the seclusion of the surrounding fells. To the north is the long ridge from Causey Pike to Whiteless Pike, a first-class walkers' highway laid out for inspection. Conspicuous in this wall of fells is the yawning bowl of Addacombe Hole, a fine hanging valley north-east from Wandope's summit. Across Rigg Beck the steep slope of Scar Crags is decorated by a pattern of contour-hugging sheep trods which contrasts sharply with a series of vertical arêtes and grooves above.

Pride of place in the outlook must be given to Newlands vale where the gentle curves of the beck are a unifying link in a landscape of isolated farmsteads. The lush green of the fields is enriched by the deeper hues of trees, with the backcloth of Catbells an echo of Causey Pike across the dale. The distant skyline includes the northern fells of Skiddaw and Blencathra with lofty Helvellyn and its satellites away to the east, but this is essentially an intimate panorama of the Newlands neighbourhood. It is a prize for discerning walkers in search of a little solitude in the midst of Lakeland's often crowded acres.

APPLETHWAITE COMMON
Some fells attract attention because of exciting outlines. Others have attractive names or reputations. There are some, however, with no obvious appeal, but you can never be sure they are without merit unless you go and find out. Usually even the least likely fells prove to be of interest in some way so that a visit prompted by curiosity can provide a worthwhile diversion. Applethwaite Common falls into this category and perhaps the best reason for seeking out its summit would be to quote Mallory: "Because it is there"—though anything less like Mallory's Everest would be hard to imagine. The Common is a gentle-looking lump of a hill near the entrance to the Troutbeck valley, the logical southern extension of the High Street range.

Applethwaite Common is topped by a grassy little ridge of hummocks overlooking the Garburn Pass, Sour Howes by name. Nearer the pass is the slightly higher Sallows, the culminating point of Kentmere Park, which is the Common's counterpart in the Kentmere scene. The road to Garburn Pass is the main walkers' thoroughfare on this piece of fell. On my shelves is a book published in 1922 with illustrations by A. Heaton Cooper, father of the Grasmere artist W. Heaton Cooper. His painting of the pass shows a wild and rugged place made all the more dark and mysterious by a squall of rain and a threatening sky. A couple of sheep stand speculatively on the brink of an apparent abyss. The author, MacKenzie MacBride, paints a picture in words of a remote, lonely spot where few people go.

Times and attitudes change. If MacKenzie MacBride were to go there today he might well wonder what had happened to his world. This is hardly the outpost he suggested in *Wild Lakeland*. A few years ago we went up there on a Sunday afternoon and there may have been at least a score of walkers of all ages on the track, enjoying the air and the pleasant sunshine of early autumn, mostly with no further ambition than to reach the top of the pass. Our own destination was Sallows. We were in no hurry and it was unlikely, we supposed, that this would be a particularly memorable walk.

We were wrong. The afternoon was one to remember, but for unusual reasons. As we left the ancient packhorse way and started up the gentle slopes of rough tussocky grass to Sallows, a strange sound echoed across the fell, the sound of the internal combustion engine. Odd, even impossible up here we thought, but there it was, unmistakably the revving of engines and near at hand too. There was nothing to be seen initially, then a jeep breasted the final rise from Troutbeck, followed by two more and a Landrover. Battered old vehicles they were, as well they might be to be subjected to that rocky road across the fells. Their progress was slow and it became even slower when the crest was reached. Outcrops of rock had to be bypassed and a steel stake was hammered into the ground so that the sturdy waggons could be winched over these more rugged sections of terrain.

This intriguing spectacle was my introduction to the

pursuit which has become known as "boggling". There has
been considerable adverse publicity, and with justification, attached to the introduction of four-wheel drive
vehicles to hill tracks here and elsewhere in the country.
Certainly complaints are justified where this kind of disturbance has become a regular occurrence, for we go to the
hills to get away from the noise of the roads—and erosion
of the ancient, unmade ways is quickly accelerated when
they are used by traffic for which they were never intended. Yet on this occasion the unexpected sight and
sound of three jeeps and a Landrover in the normally quiet
preserve of Lakeland's hills gave rise to no acid comments.
The walkers in the neighbourhood, including ourselves,
seemed to regard their presence as a bonus, something to
add interest to an afternoon on the fells. But, of course, this
was a first-time view and a novelty at that. Here was a
quartet of youthful drivers setting themselves the task of
crossing the watershed between Troutbeck and Kentmere.
They were meeting the challenge in fine fashion and we
admired the initiative of these young men who were seeking excitement in their own individual way.

There was no boggling to disturb the peace when we
visited Applethwaite Common a couple of years later. We
walked the country lanes near Ings to reach High Borrans
for a pleasant afternoon stroll across the fell, just the right
sort of walk for a family outing with young children. It was
not typical fell-walking country but patches of juniper and
chunks of rock warmed by August sunshine brought variety to the grass and heather of these easy slopes. It was a
leisurely progress. There was peace and quiet here, something that we would not have found on the popular paths
in the high season. We did see a couple of walkers on Sour
Howes, true, but only at a distance. This outing suited our
mood of the day.

From the top Kendal and Windermere were well in view
and despite a light haze the hills beyond Langdale were
clear enough to be recognized. No one disturbed us as we
scanned the wide panorama of fells and lowlands with the
long smooth line of the Pennines taking a small share of
Lakeland's glorious promise. Away to the south the salt

waters of Morecambe Bay mirrored the pale blue of the sky, watched over by the dark and distant silhouette of Blacke Combe, Cumbria's final fell.

Our sortie on Sour Howes ended with a descent through the abandoned spoils of Applethwaite Quarry, now clothed in trees and not without a certain charm of character. The large hole lends a touch of topographical excitement to this flank, more than anywhere else on the fell, adding a dash of the spice that is otherwise lacking. This had been an easy stroll for a lazy afternoon, a contrast to our usual bill of fare, but now at least we have some idea of what Applethwaite Common has to offer. Our visits may be rare but the little fell will never disappoint.

SEAT SANDAL
Seat Sandal, almost due north of Grasmere, looks down on Lakeland's most central village like a benign old guardian who stands back to watch, proud of all he sees but with the resigned air of one who is forgotten and no longer exercises any control over his protégé's affairs. The smooth, bulky fell looms large in the Grasmere scene but has never been a centre of attraction, even before the valley's traffic was whisked so briskly across his toes by the modernized road. The spotlight has always been directed towards the opposite side of the valley where Helm Crag's rocky crest, barely half the height of Seat Sandal, makes it one of the best-known mini-mountains in the whole of England. The "Lion and the Lamb" is what all the visitors want to see. Walkers in search of higher fells prefer to look further afield, to Helvellyn, or perhaps Fairfield. Although they usually cross a shoulder of Seat Sandal on the way, do they ever pause even to think of its name? Yet Grasmere's gentle custodian maintains its quiet watch, content as ever to forgo the limelight and the popular acclaim.

Smooth slopes, well proportioned too, make the fell quite pleasing to the eye, but slopes of grass stretching some 2,000 feet with hardly a break have no great appeal for walkers. I suppose the direct ascent from Grasmere is one of Lakeland's least popular outings, though the route does enjoy a certain amount of traffic as a way down for folk who have reached the top from other directions. In this respect the south ridge has much to commend it. The views of Grasmere and its superb green valley are always ahead, something worth any amount of effort to see.

As a mountain Seat Sandal has little to hide and there are hardly any secrets to unravel. Just grass—and a little rock overlooking Grisedale Hause—so it would seem that this is a dull sort of a hill, hardly worth the effort of a climb to its summit cairn unless you are a conscientious peak-bagger seeking to add yet another "top" to your collection. Yet this is not entirely true. There may be little in the way of excitement on the way up, whichever way you choose, but the summit can repay the efforts of those who do trouble to go there, and in one respect it is outstanding. Not many fells can challenge it as a viewpoint for lakes and tarns. For this reason I often think of Seat Sandal as my "Fell of Lakes".

If you include Morecambe Bay you can see a dozen stretches of water from the top, and maybe more. Admittedly, you have to move about a bit to see them all. Grisedale Tarn cannot be seen from the highest cairn but a short stroll soon brings it into view. The first time I recall noticing Alcock Tarn was from the plateau of Seat Sandal. That little pool is not obvious in mountain views but this is one place from which you can identify it without fear of error.

With the sun bright in a clear, fresh sky there can be no doubt in your mind about the reason for calling this corner of England the "Lake District". All around there are pools of light, like fragments of fallen sky, each shining with a silvery luminescence borrowed from above. Of the larger lakes Ullswater and Thirlmere are well seen, but pride of place belongs to Grasmere. The island and the incomparable setting of sylvan greenery in a ring of gentle hills make this a place apart. On the right sort of day, when summer is at its best and the popular heights are a-throng with visitors, you can hardly do better than rest your back against the old ruined wall—or better still, the south-west cairn—and survey the scene beyond your toes, at ease with the world.

Seat Sandal is the sort of place where you really can expect to find peace. You may be joined by another visitor, but probably not. The chances are that you will have the fell to yourself. As you look down on Grasmere you may try to imagine how the valley might have appeared a thousand years or more ago, before man tamed the low-lands, before the stone walls lined the hills, and when King Dunmail reigned over the land as the last king of ancient Cumbria. It must have been a wild-looking place in those days. Here, probably more than anywhere else in the fell country, the hand of man is evident as a softening influence on the landscape. The smooth slopes of Seat Sandal would be tree-covered in A.D. 945 when Dunmail was involved in the battle commemorated by the cairn on Dunmail Raise.

Popular belief suggests that the hoary pile of stones, now isolated by a short stretch of dual carriageway on the A591, is the last resting-place of the king. It is a romantic story but the evidence is against it. After his defeat by the Saxons Dunmail made his way to join an ally in Wales. Traditionally his crown and regalia were cast into Grisedale Tarn. Perhaps he did flee to the east, up the easy ravine of Raise Beck, past the tarn and down Grisedale to Patterdale. This would be a logical escape route for a party familiar with the country, as local men would be.

If King Dunmail's crown jewels really do lie at the bottom of Grisedale Tarn they are lost for ever in the silt of a thousand years. This, one of Lakeland's biggest and best-known tarns, is a third of a mile from the summit cairn of Seat Sandal. Its altitude is 1,760 feet, give or take a foot or two. Mentally adroit readers will quickly convert that figure to a third of a mile. Curiously, it is about 1,800 feet in length—again approximately a third of a mile. This is one place where coincidence is an unhappy victim of metrication!

King Dunmail's supposed walk to the tarn is simple enough to follow. From Dunmail Raise there is about 1,000 feet of easy climbing beside Raise Beck. The track is narrow but well marked and it would take an unusually incompetent man to lose himself in the confines of this gill.

It is hardly one of the district's most exciting ascents but, in spite of rather drab surroundings, the pleasant company of tumbling water is at hand to prevent boredom. Where the gradient eases the going becomes wet, for this is the gathering ground of Raise Beck, but there are much worse places and Grisedale Tarn is not far away. This is a possible way up Seat Sandal. It is simple and undemanding with a gentle slope to the summit, if you turn south near the top of the beck at the start of the marshy section, and minor outcrops of grey rock crown the skyline to tempt you onwards. They are not quite at the top of the fell but when you reach them the summit is not far away.

Raise Beck enjoys certain distinctions. The old county boundary, after accompanying the wall down from Dollywaggon Pike, turned east along the course of the stream. It can no longer separate Cumberland from Westmorland but the district boundary still takes the same line. Most of Seat Sandal belongs to the National Trust and again Raise Beck forms a useful boundary with the help of that ancient and ruined wall, which continues from Dollywaggon Pike to the top of Seat Sandal.

As you climb beside Raise Beck you are looking at one of Manchester's water supplies. The stream was diverted to feed Thirlmere when the reservoir was built, though it can still flow south to Grasmere when in spate. This fact helps to make Seat Sandal unique. Its water reaches the Irish Sea through Thirlmere's overflow—for Manchester doesn't keep it all—it heads for the Solway Firth by way of Grisedale Tarn and Ullswater; and Tongue Gill flows south to Morecambe Bay. When you remember that Manchester takes a share of Thirlmere it can be seen that Seat Sandal distributes its waters in a more widespread fashion than any other fell.

Should the name of the fell arouse curiosity remember that "Seat" is a common enough title in the north country, used for many a tract of high land. It is usual to trace the name back to the old Norse settlers whose "saetre" was a mountain pasture, or shieling. This one belonged to a fellow named Sandulf, which makes the derivation easy to recognize.

There is a little rock on the eastern flank, not much, but sufficient to maintain the pattern of these fells east of Dunmail Raise. The smooth western slopes generally give way to rougher terrain on the other side. Here the really exciting crags are further east however, on Fairfield, Hart Crag and Dove Crag, or to the north on the Helvellyn group. Seat Sandal projects west of the main line of this range of eastern fells, though it does form part of the watershed. Whatever its shortcomings in respect of crags, there is still enough rock on the wide top to encourage the cairn builders in the provision of company for the fine pyramid of stones that marks the highest point—or perhaps they have plundered the wall. In this respect, at any rate, Seat Sandal is superior to that friendly giant of a neighbour, Helvellyn, where the summit rock fractures into tiny fragments, quite unsuitable for the construction of cairns.

Maybe it is true that this is a rather dull fell by the high standards of Lakeland in general. There is certainly a lack of exciting features on its extensive grassy acres but at least here is a mountain that makes the best of what it has. No one could reasonably be disappointed by this simple fell. There is no pretence about Seat Sandal.

THE FELLS OF WYTHOP
Sale Fell and Ling Fell, a pair of amiable sentinels, mount a lazy guard over the portals of a most delightful hidden valley. The vale of Wythop seems a haven of peace, especially when viewed from the low surrounding hills which form a defensive wall against traffic and tourism in this north-western corner of the National Park. With Cockermouth a bare four miles to the west, Bassenthwaite Lake and the busy A66 just to the east and the road to Buttermere as near on the other side, there are plenty of folk on the move in the area, but Wythop remains stubbornly off the beaten track. To get there you must travel quieter by-ways and the call of better-known mountains not so very far away means that the little fells of Wythop will always be a sanctuary for walkers who seek solitude in the height of the holiday season.

The name Wythop means "the valley of the woodland" and indeed this is a place of sylvan charm, even though many of its trees are gone. That the valley is largely unsuspected by the vast majority of Lakeland's visitors is in part due to a narrow entry made even more obscure by a tumble of woodland, drawn like a curtain behind the hamlet of Wythop Mill. Over the eastern watershed the Forestry Commission has taken a hand in preserving the trees. The long-standing deciduous woodland has been allowed to remain, growing side by side with the newer coniferous plantations.

Sale Fell is the cornerstone of Wythop's fells. An isolated hill, not connected with any other high ground, it is in its own unassuming way a minor gem of the district. Choose the right day and you can enjoy pleasure quite out of proportion to the minimum of effort involved in its ascent. Here is the ideal outing for walkers whose activities are curtailed by the brake of advancing years, or the responsibilities of a young family. A pleasant, easily graded path crosses the western flank to within 400 feet of the summit, from which it can be reached by a gentle undulating stroll of less than half a mile. There are no great crags on Sale Fell, but small outcrops, often laced in white with streaks of quartz, bring variety to the terrain and quite a number of colourful boulders are exposed in the grass. They make useful seats when the family is not disposed to hurry and are all the more welcome when warmed by a bountiful sun—and that is the way it should be. On Sale Fell speed is never an asset.

Though a mere 1,170 feet in height, Sale Fell offers worthwhile views because of its fringe position, well away from any lofty screen. The finest mountain scene is of Skiddaw and its satellites. This is an unusual viewpoint and Lakeland's ancient giant has a stern and imposing look with purple-grey screes high on the western face frowning across the intervening valley. To the left, beyond the coastal plain, is the Solway Firth and Scotland's distant Criffell, looking much higher than it really is.

To the south are Lorton's pastoral acres hiding behind Sale Fell's twin, but Ling Fell is the minor partner.

Though generally of less interest it can boast one point of superiority for it is the higher fell by some fifty-five feet. Its O.S. column is surrounded by an apron of stones, whitened as an aid to aerial survey, but the paint is fading fast.

South from this summit is the wide, marshy expanse of Wythop Moss. Near the upper reaches of the Moss is a minor watershed where the waters that give this morass its spongy consistency make their reluctant decision to flow east or west. To an observer on the site it is practically impossible to detect signs of flow in any direction whatsoever, unless it be into his boots. In the event this indecision is of no consequence at all since the waters rejoin at Cockermouth, having passed either across the Vale of Lorton by way of Tom Rudd Beck and, for half a mile, the River Cocker, or alternatively through Bassenthwaite Lake. In the latter case the waters pursue a peculiarly circuitous course. Wythop Beck leaves its valley in a westerly direction, curves round Sale Fell and flows east to join Bass Lake. Half a mile to the north the River Derwent heads west again to the predestined meeting place at Cockermouth.

To add to the confusion Wythop Beck has its own twin— Beck Wythop. The streams share the same headwaters on the slopes of Lord's Seat. For perhaps a quarter of a mile their courses are virtually parallel and barely a hundred yards apart, and nothing seems more certain than the fact that they should join forces before very long. A large-scale map shows channels connecting these becks, but under the cover of plantations where it is difficult to check. However, this seems to have been a trial marriage that has been found wanting. Beck Wythop swings east to plunge impatiently down sudden slopes and enter Bass Lake after a brief but adventurous life. Wythop Beck's perverse but placid route eventually brings it to the lake a couple of miles further north. The complexities of the Wythop watercourses are more readily appreciated from a map than on the ground.

Though Wythop Beck rises on Lord's Seat that fell stands well back from the secluded valley and is usually visited from the Bassenthwaite side, where it presents an exciting front in the form of the subsidiary spur of Barf. A couple of iron fence posts mark the summit, a memento of the junction of three departed fences. There is a fair view of the upper Wythop valley from Lord's Seat but really the place is too far distant for its true self to be revealed.

The little dale has a shy, intimate quality. A year or two ago we came down from one of the lonely fells south of Wythop—Broom Fell—and passed through pastures abundant in wild flowers, truly a captivating scene. One field was deliciously bedecked in tiny wild pansies, and ditches were colourful friezes of unspoiled flora. It is fortunate that the average walker is interested only in the obvious excitements of the high fells, for mass popularity would spoil Wythop. It is likely to remain so, for only folk in sympathy with the quiet backwaters—and who are prepared to walk to find their pleasures—are going to turn that way. And if they do, let them treat this little paradise with respect and keep it as it is, a haven of peace, free from litter or noise, a place where you can truly get away from it all.

6

LOW HILLS ROUND LOWESWATER
(Backcloth of a Little Lake)

One May afternoon on the road beside Loweswater we came across a young red squirrel, no more than a baby, sitting unconcernedly by the tarmac. Sarah spotted the little fellow close under a steep bank. It was more on a level for a five-year-old's roving eyes than ours, and shaded by a small cliff of crumbling earth which had presumably proved insurmountable. Only a few yards away holiday-makers were taking their leisure at the lakeside and children were splashing happily in the water. The creature was heedless of this human activity and seemed likely to wander into the path of some passing car. When we lifted it to the shelter of trees and bracken a gentle, though insistent, hand was needed to set it moving in the right direction. The roadside plantation—from which it had most likely come—would provide a safer haven than the trees of the lake shore across the road.

We turned along the Mosser Lane but left it after a few hundred yards to join a faint trod that contours round Darling Fell between 800 and 1,000 feet, a little-known way that curves into the wide ravine of Crabtree Beck, where a neat sheepfold displays a sense of economy on the part of its unknown architect. Sturdy walls abut a tiny crag whose rocky face forms one side of the enclosure. The track to the sheepfold, short and not at all well marked, is a delight to trace, a scenic traverse much better known to sheep than humans. The Loweswater panorama is well displayed and the Loweswater Fells stand proudly at the far side of the lake with noble Mellbreak imposing a dominating presence on the group, yet despite Mellbreak's call for attention the eye is inevitably drawn to the grand façade of Grasmoor across the Buttermere valley.

Loweswater and its surroundings make a pleasant, pastoral scene where the signs of careful husbandry are evident on all sides. The place attracts an appreciative tourist clientele and seems to accept this sort of attention with a shrug of the shoulders as though to say, "This is how we are and this is how we stay." There is a sense of continuity about the area, an unchanging detachment that has lasted through the centuries and appears unlikely to alter as this century comes to its close. There seems to be no reason why the next millennium should be any different from the last. Tourists may come and tourists may go but Loweswater remains the same. Even the fleeting invasion of B.B.C. Television, when the programme *One Man and His Dog* recorded the skills of sheepdog handling, and brought a temporary national fame, has left little mark.

The surrounding hills are on the small scale. There is no land in the immediate neighbourhood that tops the 2,000-foot mark. The highest summit of Blake falls well short of that figure, a mere, 1,878 feet, and Mellbreak, the only fell with any aspirations towards popularity, stands a couple of hundred feet short of that. These hills to the south of the lake go by the collective name of the Loweswater Fells. They tend to be more characteristic of Lakeland than their slaty companions to the north, though even there the Loweswater slopes are steep enough to make sure that the little valley remains scenically in keeping with the best that the district can offer.

Our walk from Loweswater took us to the summit of Low Fell, some 400 feet above the sheepfold near Crabtree Beck. There are two rises, either of which might claim to be the highest point, but the smooth curves of the northern top lack the character of its southern counterpart which is in any case a better viewpoint and that, for me, is the end of the argument. The vista is worth the effort of climbing a hill twice the height. Buttermere's valley with its surround of magnificent fells sets the scene. With so much excellence around it is not easy to pick out an outstanding feature. Mellbreak looks good—as it does from most angles—and Grasmoor shows its proudest aspect. Yet the most memorable mountain picture in my mind is at the head of Buttermere where Haystacks stands in front of Great Gable and cheekily apes the formidable outline. The gentle acres of Lorton are a contrast to the stirring display of high country to the south and east. It is a contrast to the benefit of either extreme.

Low Fell is a cornerstone to an extensive range of modest, grassy hills but the gap shows several other individual summits, mostly of similar height. Together they give the impression of being outsiders, trying to get into Lakeland by the back door while no one is looking. Two of them compete for seniority. Low Fell is a grand viewpoint but the Ordnance Surveyors have not given us its true altitude and we can only make a guess based on the published contours. A geographically more satisfying centrepiece is Fellbarrow. The height is 1,364 feet here, according to the last pre-metric assessment of the cartographers, and most ordinary folk will be quite happy to accept this as the summit of these north-of-Loweswater hills.

On a pleasant spring afternoon we chose to walk the Whinfell Road with Fellbarrow as our target. Dusty undulations in the stony track made us feel secure from the intrusion of cars and the luxurious growth of the hedge on either side was bespangled with the delicate wayside flowers of the early season. As we ambled unhurriedly along the thought crossed my mind, "Were the roads like this before the coming of motor transport?" Much as I like to reach for the tops it was this ancient bridleway connecting Lorton with Mosser and Pardshaw that made this an afternoon to remember. The Mosser end of the lane was a particular delight. Twinkling highlights seen through dancing leaves showed where sun-sprayed clouds chased across the sky, and in the arboreal shade a frieze of flowers on either hand suggested a fairy grotto leading to the sunshine of the fell.

But in spite of the sun it was cool, and a strong breeze from the north-east brought a chill when we left the shelter of the trees. As the lane emerged from its sylvan drapery there came a reminder that here is the very edge of the fell country and the view across the lowlands held a dis-

tant sparkle where the Solway meets the sea. Nearer were
farmers going about their business. Sheep and lambs
needed attention even if a trio of strangers could find time
to take a leisurely walk on the Whinfell Road, but we saw
no other people that day.

Neglect by the fell-walking fraternity is one of the attractions of Fellbarrow's happy little company. There is a
feeling that folk turn their backs on the hill and the gentle
slopes above Lorton seem a forgotten land. Even those
whose home was once here have forsaken the place, as
ruined farmsteads proclaim. One of these we passed was
Hatteringill, a tumble of old stones and now a natural
collecting point for water. In its day it commanded a fine
view, but views do not feed hungry families, rather
Lorton's green vale was always a reminder of lusher
pastures bordering the fell country. Hatteringill could
never compete with richer farmlands not all that far away.

The higher slopes above Hatteringill have a scattering
of decrepit trees and the upper reaches give the eastern
side of the fell the appearance of a balding hedgehog.
There must have been extensive tree cover at one time. In
fact much of this country was kept as a deer park in the
Middle Ages, being a part of the Copeland Forest, though
early documents show that local people were granted certain rights of pasturage on what was mainly a huntsman's
preserve. Perhaps the trees were once part of the ancient
natural forest but they are now stunted wrecks of their
former selves. They are no obstacle to ascent and they are
just about the only natural feature of interest in the immediate vicinity of the summit.

The ancient trees overlook the small, secluded dell of
Meregill Beck. This is Fellbarrow's hidden valley, an almost secret hollow peacefully tucked away in a fold in the
hills. An old drove road wends its way through this lonely
recess and across a shoulder of Sourfoot Fell, where the
modest altitude of these little hills is emphasized by a farm
gate across the track on the ridge north from Low Fell. A
pleasant way up, this, with a gradient compassionate to
wind and limb, and two delightfully engineered zigzags to
take any suggestion of sting out of the final rise from

Meregill Beck. Nearby is Watching Crag whose name is clear evidence of its local reputation as a viewpoint. The Meregill zigzags stand out boldly when viewed from the tattered forest remnants of Fellbarrow.

Generally, the eastern side of this small group of hills is more interesting than the western flank, though down by Mosser Beck the trees and pastures have a charm of their own. But this is farming country, a land of cattle as much as of sheep, and there is nothing to appeal to any self-respecting fell walker in a place where the real hills are so obviously a long way away. An old, grassed-over track leading down that way suggests another drove road, and the ruins of Crosshill spell out the same message as Hatteringill and present a stark, forlorn appearance in the gloom of evening. On the spring afternoon when we were down there the cattle-churned mud near the beck was frozen into ankle-wrecking craters by a hard, day-long frost—and this was the 29th of May. It felt like winter, and that night there was thick snow on the fells.

A feature of Fellbarrow and its immediate neighbours north of Loweswater is that they are defended to a large extent by private farmlands and there are not so many rights of way giving access to the open fell. This is less the case south of the lake where rights of way are clearly indicated. They are more used to visitors here and the most obvious barrier is the lake itself. Yet it is worth remembering that farm land represents someone's livelihood and farmers have every right to feel aggrieved when they see thoughtless walkers taking unnecessary short cuts across their fields, with the possible consequence of damage to crops, walls and fences, or disturbance of livestock. In any case it is rank bad manners to treat the property of others in such cavalier fashion. There is plenty of freedom to walk at will on the open fell country without making free with private pastures. Courtesy and consideration should be the watchwords for all fell walkers.

These thoughts spring from memories of a recent walk over Blake Fell and Burnbank Fell, where the route recommended in a guide book had been overruled at the outset by signs directing walkers into an adjacent field.

There were good reasons for the alteration, which was not detrimental to the walk in any way, and our immediate reaction was of sympathy for the farmer. It is a situation which must be repeated on countless locations throughout the country, where farmers are obliged to accept the intrusion of strangers on their land whether they like it or not, and with no advantage to themselves whatsoever, simply because a right of way exists. The fact is that most minor rights of way originated as a result of usage by local people from time immemorial. They just grew naturally as useful ways between various places in a locality and were used primarily by people whom the tenant or landowner knew personally. They were developed through mutual respect and not with the leisure activities of modern society in mind.

There can be no criticism of any minor diversions in the Loweswater neighbourhood and in any case they have no effect on the main objective of most walkers, whose intention is usually a walk round the lake and a visit to the groves of Holme Wood. There are some beautiful ways through the trees here, worth a couple of hours of anybody's time. They can be followed at several levels. A particular favourite of mine is the upper track which visits Holme Force, where Holme Beck is a cascade of sparkling champagne as it tumbles down rocky ledges in a bower of trees. You hear it long before you see it and at first suspect the rustle of the breeze in the leaves if you have no suspicion of its presence. After the gentle pull up the hillside from the lake there is every inclination to rest for a few minutes where the bridge crosses the little ravine. Not so far beyond there is—or was—a neat arch where a fallen tree rests across the track. A drapery of ferns and mosses adds a touch of the picturesque to one of nature's follies.

These trees clothe the lower slopes of Blake and Burnbank Fells. Blake Fell's major importance is its height, for it has the highest summit of the group. For this reason it must command some attention, though many visitors are likely to be satisfied when they reach Carling Knott at the end of the north-east ridge. That would certainly be true for members of a football club from the south, whose man-

ager had them running up there during training sessions
when they were presented with a pre-season "holiday" at
Loweswater! The lake views are good from Carling Knott
but it is certainly worth the small amount of extra effort
needed to reach Blake. The crossing is mainly on grass but
a tiny edge of rock on the left adds a little interest to the
first quarter of a mile.

The Loweswater Fells—Burnbank, Blake, Gavel Fell
and Hen Comb—generally give decent walking on grass
and are pleasant outings in good weather. Mellbreak completes the quintet, but Mellbreak is rather special, a mini-
mountain of distinction separated from its fellows by the
wide, wet valley of Mosedale. It is a fell of genuine character and deservedly takes its place in a later chapter. Its
immediate partner is Hen Comb, a gently rising grassy
ridge with a knob of rock, Little Dodd, at mid-height. Hen
Comb is more in character with the general pattern of the
Loweswater Fells and Mosedale is the moat that marks its
eastern margin.

Mosedale as a title is always a warning to any walker
and, of all the Lakeland Mosedales, this could well be the
loneliest. Wherever you see the name on the map you can
usually expect to find marshy land and here is one of the
boggiest of the lot, especially at its head. The place has a
reputation, and not without reason. There is no wonder
that it is so rarely frequented. A dreary sort of wasteland is
what you might expect to find, and if the sky is overcast or
rain is sweeping over the hills you will not be disappointed. But even the most unlikely places can have their
moments and if the weather is right, and your mood is
receptive, even this Mosedale can be worth a visit. The
valley is a sun-trap. We have been there in brilliant
sunshine to enjoy the spaciousness of a wide, open-ended
trough with a fine expanse of blue sky above our heads.
Mind you, we did keep away from the worst of the morass,
and even then the midges and other inevitable flying insects made their presence felt. That part of our exploration
was an experience to forget!

The nearest that most folk come to experiencing the
bogs of Mosedale is when they visit Scale Force. The

waterfall has a reputation to maintain as the highest in Lakeland. It is a "must" for many of Buttermere's visitors and there is no doubt that it is impressive because of the close approach that is not only possible, but necessary, yet most people that I have spoken to seem to find the journey there more memorable than the objective. A wealth of unsuitable footwear has been reduced almost to pulp by the juicy defences of Scale Force.

Lakeland's highest waterfall is not set in the Loweswater Fells but it faces them from the lower slopes of Red Pike and Starling Dodd, with the oozy upland marsh of upper Mosedale keeping walkers to that side of the valley. It is difficult to imagine that the track here was once a regular way between Buttermere and Ennerdale. It is still listed in some publications as one of the Lakeland foot passes. Perhaps travellers in days long past were more insensible to the kind of discomfort that only wearers of wellington boots can shrug off with a smile, or it could be that in those days the route took a more sensible line and was regularly maintained.

Floutern Tarn, near the head of the pass, has a name of Norse origin and means "boggy tarn", which seems appropriate enough in the circumstances. The valley is choked with morainic material, an effective curb to drainage. The tarn is about 300 yards long and quite narrow. It is one of the least-known tarns and is the final limit of the Loweswater Fells in this direction. Hen Comb and Gavel Fell reach down to touch its northern shore. We once came this way in late October when gloriously sunny weather caressed the fells, a touch of summer that would be hard to beat in July. We spent a pleasant hour with sandwiches and Sunday papers at the nearby summit of Great Borne—sunbathing! This says something about the vagaries of the English climate, especially when compared with the snow that opened the month of June in another year. But you come to expect this sort of variety if you walk the fells with any regularity.

7

GATEWAYS TO HIGH PLACES
(Ullock Pike; Loadpot Hill; Bessyboot; Causey Pike)

There are some fells, often quite small in themselves, which feel the passage of countless feet because they occupy the position of stepping stones to a highland hinterland—and there are many more which perhaps ought to do so but tend to be ignored, either because they lie at the wrong side of their parent mass as far as the usual point of popular access is concerned, or because they are obscure and unlikely specimens that most walkers prefer to miss. Sometimes these hills are worthwhile objectives in their own right and just a few are widely recognized as such. The finest example in this category is Causey Pike which must rank high in the esteem of most fell walkers. One that would undoubtedly be included here is Catbells, were it not also a favourite for family outings and just could not be left out of Chapter 3. Many others may have their advocates but find a slot under a different heading, and in some cases there may be disappointment that a personal favourite has no place in the book at all. Unfortunately pressure of space must of necessity limit the choice. Of those included here, perhaps Bessyboot will cause the greatest surprise but I hope its presence will be fully justified in the pages that follow, so that it may be accepted into the brotherhood of "Gateways to High Places".

ULLOCK PIKE
Ullock Pike must for ever remain subservient to Skiddaw. The Grand Old Man of the Lakeland fells—Skiddaw is composed of the oldest rock of the district and is the highest of these slaty mountains—dominates this part of

the Lake District and stands proud of Ullock Pike by the best part of a thousand feet so that popular views place the minor fell in true perspective as a foothill of a compact mountain group. The Pike is merely a point on a ridge, part of the build-up to the fourth highest mountain in England.

Yet if you view the group from the village of Bassenthwaite or, better still, from Ouse Bridge at the foot of Bass Lake, then Ullock Pike comes into its own. In this view the secret recesses of Southerndale show a clear separation from the parent mountain. This little hill may be built of the same basic materials as Skiddaw but there the resemblance ends. A long, narrow ridge curls round to a neat col behind Carl Side and the Pike takes the form of a neat pyramid—in this end-on view— with a steep flank on either side. The ridge presents a clear and unequivocal invitation to all fell walkers. Surely if it faced south-east instead of north-west and had its roots in the vale of Keswick, this approach to Skiddaw would rank as one of the most popular ascents in Lakeland.

When Skiddaw has his cap on and great wreaths of cloud roll down to fill the trough of Southerndale, then is the time when Ullock Pike assumes an air of real individuality. With the vast banks of Skiddaw masked in misty anonymity the Pike becomes Bassenthwaite's personal fell and lays claim to the little village at its foot in a way that the more distant giant can never manage.

Geographically Ullock Pike is of little moment. It is merely the point at which the steepness of the ridge eases and, after the slightest of depressions, it takes the best part of a mile to climb the remaining 400 feet to Carl Side where a col connects with the main mountain mass. This high ridge, consistently over 2,000 feet, is Longside Edge. In the middle reaches it rises to 2,405 feet and is known as Long Side, a name of convenience borrowed from the flank overlooking Bassenthwaite Lake, as a glance at the map will confirm. The western slope which sweeps down to the lake is hardly visible to travellers on the road below for most of its length because of the continuous cloak of trees provided by Dodd Wood. The Forestry Commission has completely clothed the minor outlier, Dodd, in evergreen but the plantations will never reach the roof-top of the ridge. Forward planning is beginning to bear fruit here and a policy of large-scale landscape gardening is gradually softening the harsher effects of the plantations.

Over the ridge the eastern slopes are bare, rough and even more steeply pitched. Here is the shy, quiet valley of Southerndale, almost a secret valley and seen to advantage only from the ridge. It is little frequented by walkers for in this land of peaks they naturally prefer the tops. It does present an easy way off the Skiddaw group if you are bound for Bassenthwaite but who would choose this in preference to Longside Edge? From Skiddaw Little Man there is a splendidly inviting prospect of Ullock Pike and the Edge, an outline vaguely reminiscent of lonely Suilven in the far north-west of Scotland. There can be no finer recommendation than that! Should you choose to descend to Bassenthwaite by this route you will not be long in realizing the wisdom of your decision. After negotiating the inevitable rough scree slopes to reach Carlside Col there is nothing but joy ahead.

Incidentally, the col sports one of the few tarns of the slaty northern fells. It is tiny, an insignificant pool with the curious decoration of a cairn growing out of the water right in the middle. At least it was there the last time I passed by, but you never can tell. These creations come and go. There are plenty of irrelevant cairns on and about Skiddaw, and throughout the district for that matter, but this one must take the crown. Surely it called for efforts above and beyond the call of duty—or else a well-developed sense of humour!

The Edge seems strangely out of place in the Skiddaw group. It would be more at home across the lake where the glorious ridges of north-west Lakeland lie like gigantic frozen ripples between the vales of Keswick and Buttermere. It has much in common with those Newlands fells, but there the names of Causey Pike and Grisedale Pike exert a magnetic influence to bring walkers back time and again. It is no exaggeration to suggest that for one visit to Ullock Pike you can count a dozen to Causey

Pike, and that may well be an underestimation. My own
experience bears this out for my own visits agree with this
ratio. The reason is no mystery. The challenging shape of
Causey Pike is plainly visible from a popular centre and is
the stepping stone to a wealth of fine country. Ullock Pike
is tucked away in an outlying corner and leads uncompromisingly to Skiddaw and nothing else. Yet ignore it
and you are the loser.

The little slaty cliffs that arrest the smooth flow of the
fellside into Southerndale are quite impressive—in this
area. Certainly they impress in a way that nothing on
Causey Pike can manage and they are daunting enough to
place the flank out of bounds to all but the most determined of walkers.

Some years ago I sat on Ullock Pike enjoying a quiet
pipe in the later afternoon sunshine of early August. A
small family group was approaching from Carl Side when
for no apparent reason the leader made an abrupt right-
angled turn and plunged down towards Southerndale. I
watched, amazed. Within minutes father was almost beside the beck while his famly, including young children,
was strung out in disarray with two of them in obvious
difficulties. One little girl made very slow progress and
soon became cragfast on a small outcrop about halfway
down. Evidently help would be needed but as I set out to
lend a hand the danger at last became apparent to the
watching father, and he retraced his steps to give belated
aid. Eventually he had his flock reassembled by Southerndale Beck and he led the way down the valley. Why he
should choose so unorthodox a route with a magnificent
ridge in prospect is hard to understand, but that is an
enigma of no consequence at all when set beside the lack of
consideration for those children in need of careful guid-
ance over difficult ground, assuming it necessary to take
them there in the first place. I returned to my perch on
Ullock Pike musing on the foolhardiness of some visitors
to the fells.

As I refilled my pipe a gentle scraping sound edged its
way into my perception. Turning quickly I came face to
face with a bold and woolly countenance and for a moment

it seemed that I was about to be pitched over the brink to join the objects of my erstwhile deliberations. The determined ewe stood her ground, apparently seeking a hand-out. Some folk are too free with their sandwiches, it would seem, but this old girl would get nothing from me. In any case my lunch packet was empty, the final crumbs having been consumed ages ago on Skiddaw. After a brief sniff at my hand she evidently decided that tobacco is a poor substitute for a tasty bit of bread and she wandered off with many a backward glance that spoke of regret. Man's inhumanity to sheep was the message told by those large, baleful eyes.

Before leaving this delectable spot I took a last look round. You get a good view of the lake from here. There are not many places where you can follow a high ridge with water consistently in view in this fashion. When the yachts sally forth from the foot of the lake there is a pleasantly restful quality about the scene. Bassenthwaite Lake is one of the least-known major waters of the district, despite its close proximity to Keswick. In general its shore stands well back from the road and is little seen. From Longside Edge and Ullock Pike the shoreline of bays and promontories takes the eye. There is one of Cumbria's Bownesses down there, and a Bowness Bay too, but anything less like Windermere's famous and crowded resort would be hard to imagine.

I looked for and pinpointed the lonely little Bass church and then glanced across the water to the conifers of Thornthwaite Forest knowing that the scene was echoed on this side of the valley a few hundred feet below my boots but out of sight from where I stood. The main impression was not of plantations, however. This is a pastoral panorama, a pattern in which fields seem almost incidental to their boundary hedges. Trees certainly take a large share of the outlook but it is a deciduous network that holds the eye, not one of evergreen.

Too soon it was time to move. The easy descent of the widening ridge was a delight, with the late sunshine glinting on a distant silvery Solway and the shadowed hills of the Galloway peninsula closing the far horizon. I went down past The Watches, a curious collection of boulders standing sentinel near the foot of the ridge, and so I reached the road where an unexpected but pleasant surprise awaited. My wife drove into view, judging my arrival with superb timing and the last mile or so of road walking became a couple of minutes' ride. The day ended in style!

LOADPOT HILL

Loadpot Hill, land of sheep and ponies, rests quietly on the north-eastern periphery of Lakeland. It is not a fell for folk of gregarious disposition and even in August I have found the area almost devoid of human life. The fell offers little in the way of dramatically exciting scenery, just a rolling prairie that delights the sheep, and the ponies whose special preserve it is, but it none the less exerts a peculiar attraction all its own. It occupies an extensive tract of land and takes under its wing a number of satellites which hold a great deal of individual character. If you climb Loadpot Hill for its own sake, rather than treating it as a gateway to the High Street range, you can include these outliers and experience a sense of minor exploration on the verge of the Lakeland hills.

The summit of Loadpot Hill occupies a position where the northern foothills of High Street begin to come together to form the beginnings of the long, high-level ridge that delights lovers of extended mountain days. The Romans knew the place—their road from Ambleside to Broughton passed west of the summit—but even they were newcomers to Loadpot Hill. The ancient Britons had long-distance tracks before Caesar stepped on our shores and their routes kept to the highest land, well away from the valley bottoms which were undrained swampy wildernesses, not cleared of trees as we know them today. Celtic remains have been found along them, including stone axes from Langdale, and it is easy to visualize the prehistoric artisans of Langdale despatching their goods in this direction in their quest for trade.

There may be no evidence of these Ancients along the High Street ridge, though surely they knew their way along it and in such a remote country the Romans would be happy to follow a proven route. Students of Roman history in the British Isles have investigated the authenticity of High Street as a Roman road by digging out a section on the northern slopes of Loadpot Hill. Their findings seem to verify the tradition for the results were consistent with known methods of Roman road construction. But there is little to see to suggest a made way these days, just a good fell-walkers' track leading to high places. It is the one place on the fell where you are likely to meet with a fellow walker. Elsewhere a lonely, rarely trodden expanse of grass and gentle gradients leads down to pastoral lands on the eastern fringe of the district, where the old road over Shap Fell begins the long pull to the summit. The River Lowther winds through the picturesque acres of Lowther Park with its modern wildlife country park, offering a splendid opportunity to observe temperate animals wandering free. Here is a fine place for families to enjoy an off-day between jaunts on the fells.

Loadpot Hill is part of the Lowther estates. It is a wild-life park in its own right and you don't pay for admission either. Apart from the ubiquitous sheep you are more than likely to meet with Fell ponies grazing peacefully on these grasslands. The red deer of Martindale recognize no arbitrary boundaries and are quite at liberty to wander here too, and many birds and other small creatures enjoy a freedom from the disturbance that makes them less likely to be seen on the more popular fells.

The Fell pony is a most characteristic animal of these quiet upland pastures. He has the freedom to range as wild as the wind, though his freedom is no more genuine than that of the sheep, for each pony is some one's property. He has a rough and shaggy coat which gives a wild appearance when outlined against the sky, but his looks belie his true docility. Quite large, he has a strength that makes him an excellent working animal, a strength that stands him in good stead when the colder weather arrives. That thick warm coat comes into its own as a barrier against the rigours of an upland winter and the ponies will graze up to the skyline in the coldest of weather. The sight of these sturdy beasts brings a positive thrill of excitement, which may seem strange when you consider that ponies and horses are a commonplace feature of our countryside, but the Fell pony is something special and a genuine part of the Lake District scene.

The summit of Loadpot Hill is much to a pony's liking, a gentle grassy promenade with the main track avoiding the highest ground at 2,201 feet. The small and lonely cairn has in recent years been granted company in the shape of a large O.S. column solidly constructed from colourful rock. There was once a shooting lodge near the summit. It had the grandiose name of Lowther House—which betrayed its origins and ownership—but when its useful days were over it was dismantled, apart from the stonework. This was left intact so that Loadpot Hill was adorned by a fireplace with a tall chimney stack, a curiosity that stood for many years and made the place unique. It collapsed in 1973 leaving many a walker sad at the loss of an unimportant but eccentric landmark.

Overlooking the lowest reach of Ullswater are the rocky bastions of Bonscale Pike and Arthur's Pike, two northern subsidiaries of Loadpot Hill which act as a foil to the more pastoral lands across the water. Bonscale Pike is the site of three proud beacons, one an excellent craftsman's construction, but they are all conspicuous on the skyline as seen from Ullswater. This minor fell has a lasting place in my affections because it was our daughter's first Lakeland summit. The occasion is permanently etched on my memory for we chose a day when summer was at its hottest and Sarah made the ascent on my back. The abrupt Fusedale flank, east of Howtown, can never have seemed steeper.

BESSYBOOT

As a gateway to high places Bessyboot is obscure, to say the least, but for the purist it is the logical beginning of a ridge route that leads to the highest land in the country. I suppose it is a route not often considered except by the *cognoscenti* for it is a challenging proposition, not to be undertaken lightly by the average walker, but those who start out for Scafell Pike by climbing on to the ridge at

Stonethwaite will feel tremendous satisfaction—if they stay the course.

Most usually this start is omitted and the ridge gained by following Comb Gill to reach the skyline at Comb Door, north of Glaramara, but that is not really playing the game. In any case such an alternative deprives the walker of certain highlights which make the effort worthwhile, though in truth there is little time for a leisurely enjoyment of such features so early in a day which is bound to be long and arduous. If you want to have a good look at this little fell it is best to forget the Scafells and content yourself with a pleasant perambulation on one of Lakeland's least-visited tops. You can make a full day of it for there is plenty to explore in this small corner of Borrowdale.

Bessyboot is really only a small part of Rosthwaite Fell and not even the highest point—which is in doubt anyway—but the name is too good to be ignored and much more fascinating than the rather prosaic Rosthwaite Fell, though the latter is preferred by more than a few walkers. If you make the climb from the Stonethwaite valley, which you should although it hardly seems an obvious proposition from there, you will gravitate towards the neat top of Bessyboot which seems the most natural climax to the northern half of the fell. Beyond is a somewhat confusing land of bumps and dips which does not sort itself out until you reach Comb Door on the fringe of Glaramara. If you wish to savour the taste of being lost in Lakeland try crossing this bewildering area in mist without a compass—or with one for that matter. Your chances will still be high.

There is one obvious weakness in the defences of Bessyboot above Stonethwaite. The gash of Stanger Gill reaches the valley in trees about 400 yards beyond the hamlet. It looks steep, and at first glance intimidating, but there are no problems and on a fine day it gives a pleasant ascent with excellent views to reward any backward glance. One grassy clearing that I remember with affection is a tiny verdant platform projecting from the steep fellside where you look out over tree tops at your feet to a beautiful prospect of Borrowdale behind the cottages of

Rosthwaite. There it lies, a miniature Eden in a framework of leaves, a perfect composition in a bowl of hills that will produce ecstasies of delight for any camera enthusiast.

Stanger Gill is good too, with ravine scenery at its best, but the most interesting gill on the fell is Comb Gill, not so much for itself but for what it contains. It is a hanging valley, typical of its kind, and it is the natural boundary of Rosthwaite Fell as a whole on this western side. Near the head of the gill, half-way up the flank of Rosthwaite Fell, are Doves' Nest Caves, the only notable natural caves in volcanic Lakeland. They seem to be the result of a rockslip on a grand scale, dating from some time in the distant geological past when Doves' Nest Crag tried to shed a portion of its anatomy. A large slice of the lower buttress has subsided and come to rest slightly lower down the slope. Within this collapsed structure is a series of dark and dusty holes. Rock climbers have found interest in the layout, enjoying the unusual sensation of "indoor" climbing in the great outdoors.

Recently Doves' Nest Crag has shuddered again. A fall of rock has made the caves highly dangerous, even for experts, and the advice to all is "Please Keep Out". This has never been a place for walkers, who lack the specialized techniques required to tackle the crags, though bolder individuals have been able to undertake circumspect reconnaissance. On the odd occasion when I scrambled about the portals of Doves' Nest Caves I decided to leave deeper exploration until an unspecified later date. Now I can safely forget the half-hearted promise without any loss of face.

Not far above Doves' Nest Crag is Rosthwaite Cam, the most distinctive top on the southern half of the fell. It is not the highest point but it is certainly the most impressive of the many rises that attempt to dissociate themselves from the otherwise undistinguished upland in the vicinity. Rosthwaite Cam has an advantage over its competitors: rock, and that is a real consideration as far as red-blooded wanderers are concerned. It even has a look of impregnability from some angles, in the eyes of simple fell walkers, but from the south its tiny cairn may be reached without difficulty.

Between Rosthwaite Cam and Bessyboot, in a bewildering area of hillocks and marsh, is the lonely Tarn at Leaves. It empties into the Langstrath valley by way of Tansy Gill, down one of the least-visited fellsides in all Lakeland. A lonely fellside, a lonely tarn and a lonely fell; this little corner is in the middle of some of the most frequented fell-walking country in Cumbria but its fate is to be forgotten. Perhaps its offerings are for the most part modest, but never forget Doves' Nest Caves and Stanger Gill. The caves bring a taste of fame, for they are known by many who have never walked the fell and maybe never intend to, but the secrets of Stanger Gill are enjoyed by just the few. For me this will always be the best part of an odd little wedge of high land, a good reason for forgetting the Scafells and for enjoying a pleasant little fell for itself.

CAUSEY PIKE

From the hamlet of Stair, Causey Pike looks every bit as challenging as a miniature Matterhorn. On an overcast day it is a defiant challenge; when the sun shines the abrupt sweep of rugged fell seems to reach out and grasp you, but it is a friendly grasp, more of a handshake than a threatening fist. The first time I saw Causey Pike I knew that here was a fell that just had to be climbed. Its magnetic attraction reached across Derwentwater to the streets of Keswick from where its beckoning shape was glimpsed through a gap in the buildings. And that is how visitors notice it for the first time, or perhaps it stops them in their tracks down by the boat landings or at Friar's Crag. Here is one peak that genuinely deserves to be called "Pike", much more so than many another fell of like name. It looks every inch a mountain though barely 2,000 feet in height.

In fact Causey Pike is the first—or final—upsurge on one of the best-loved ridges in the Cumbrian mountains, echoing on a larger scale the similar sculpture of Catbells at the other side of the vale of Newlands. As the first step to higher things beyond it must be one of the most climbed of

Lakeland's smaller fells, yet its shape makes sure that it is hardly subservient to the comparative giants presiding over the hinterland. Though they may be higher they tend to be upstaged by this usurper with the crinkled crown. Seen end-on the fell stabs a cocky thumb at the sky, but a side view shows a more characteristic shape. Five knuckles of rock contest their claims to the supreme status, giving the outline so easily recognized as it jostles for position in views from so many summits, but that final thumb has no competitor in the summit stakes. Resting above a plunging rocky stairway, it is a fitting climax to a grand little mountain.

You can hardly avoid the top if you set out to walk the ridge to Eel Crag and beyond. On the face of it there would appear to be only two reasonable lines of approach: along the ridge in either direction. However, a brief check shows that I have reached its bald pate from no fewer than six different starting points—some several times—so though the hill holds a few secrets from the common gaze there is scope for exploration even on this limited acreage if you have the initiative to look for something a little different.

The most popular way up is obvious from afar. The track is a scar across the northern flank from Stonycroft Bridge to Sleet Hause, then it turns to climb the nose of the fell and a short, easy scramble leads directly to the summit. You could almost climb it by touch, blindfolded. Two of us once chose to wander up that way at midnight. Rain, turning to sleet and hail, brought a reminder that August and the popular conception of summer weather do not necessarily go hand in hand, and a tot of rum to celebrate the ascent brought an illusion of warmth as we peered through streaming eyes in the direction of Derwentwater. Occasional specks of light seen between gaps in drifting mist could well have been the lights of Keswick, across the lake, or perhaps car headlights on the A66. We did not stay long enough to decide but hurried down, wet yet happy, to a warming brew and the comfort of waiting beds. Friends—who remained so in spite of doubts voiced against our sanity—were relieved to welcome our return.

The first few hundred yards above Stonycroft Bridge hold a maze of tracks from which you can pick and choose at will before settling down for the steady plod to the top, but the other side of the ridge above Rigg Beck is in contrast virtually trackless. This is Birkrigg Brow. The vestige of a track does lead down from Sleet Hause but it soon fades away, unless it has become better marked since last I went that way. Yet it was this hillside that we selected for a first sortie on Causey Pike many years ago. Two of us took the boat across Derwentwater, climbed over the Catbells ridge at Hause Gate and trotted across Newlands to the foot of our objective. We reached the highest point on this group of hills, Grasmoor, then walked down Coledale to Braithwaite, arriving just as the inn opened its doors. The invitation was too welcome to ignore and with hardly a pause we strode inside. Rarely can hospitality have been more acceptable after a hot and dusty day among the fells.

This was a splendid day blessed with the warm sunshine of true summer, a fine walk with much that was memorable, but for me the highlight was not a brief moment on a mountain top, rather a timeless interlude on the slopes of Causey Pike when we settled on a warm bed of sweet-scented heather half-way up Birkrigg Brow. Time was forgotten as we relaxed and listened to the gentle hum of bees going about their business on a vast sea of vivid purple. We enjoyed a sense of the pioneering spirit resting there on a seemingly untrodden mountainside. Below were walkers on the path to Buttermere beside Rigg Beck. Cars crawled round the hairpin at the mouth of the valley, bound for the same destination by way of Newlands Hause. Above our heads would be other travellers setting out in a similar direction along one of the best-loved ridges in Lakeland, but all this activity was a world away. For the moment time itself seemed at rest and no one would disturb our island of peace. The image remains, of sun-scented air, the rich hue of the heather and the hills of Newlands all around; and of the sweat drying on our shirts. Moments like these come close to explaining the attraction of the hills.

Less than a mile west of our resting place, almost below the summit of the Pike, is a small patch of trees related to the Keskadale Oaks over the next ridge on Ard Crags. The Birkrigg Oaks are similarly supposed to be a piece of relict woodland. It is often forgotten that the bare fellsides of the present day are not a natural landscape; that man is responsible for the clearance of the forests of England. The Keskadale and the Birkrigg Oaks both lie approximately between the 1,000 and 1,500 contours and blend with the fellside so that unless you know they are there and look for them you might easily pass, unaware of their presence.

I have reached the top of Causey Pike directly up the fellside from the Stonycroft mine track, a bee-line crossing from Outerside. Another time we met the fell head-on, climbing over Rowling End and scrambling over rocks on the way. Then there is the track up the right-hand side of Rowling End, much more worthwhile than the boot-eroded main track from Stonycroft Bridge. These outings had Causey Pike as a prelude, but the knobbly summit has also provided a happy conclusion to a day on the hills. It is a particularly satisfying final peak on the high-level cross-ing from Buttermere and often enough we have enjoyed the carefree romp along the ridge from Eel Crag. The route is wonderfully direct with a real feeling of high places as you stride along visiting each summit in turn. On either hand is an immediate plunge to a deep strath and as you come to Causey Pike the bedrock kisses the highland air in a final gesture against the surrounding valleys.

The view is as good as from any 2,000-foot top you can name. Newlands' lush green pattern backed by the low-land bowl of Keswick is the outstanding feature in the outlook, for this terminal point of the ridge juts out like the prow of a ship with only the short projection of Rowling End between you and the lowland panorama. The back-cloth of fells is good to look at too. It might be thought that Skiddaw would hold the stage but really the finest moun-tain scene is centred on the head of Newlands—and a glance to the west holds its own fascination. You see the long line of the ridge stretching back to a final knob at Whiteless Pike above Buttermere, a ribbon of high country suspended above the trough of Rigg and Sail Becks. Immediately south of Rigg Beck is the crest of Ard Crags and Knott Rigg, mimicking this greater line of fells like a shadow. Even the initial step of Rowling End has its counterpart in Aikin Knott.

Causey Pike is popular both for itself and as the first step to greater things. Yet it is surprising how many times we have managed to have the summit to ourselves. In all conditions—sun, rain, wind or snow; day and night—it has extended a welcome. It holds few secrets, no tarns, no waterfalls, no becks unshared by any other fell, but it is a friendly little peak. I have a genuine affection for the hill and it must always find a place in any list of favourites.

Typical of my memories is a late October day when we sheltered from the wind in the hollow behind the summit. Despite the vigorous breeze we observed the ritual of a summit pipe. I accepted the offer of a drink but numbed fingers fumbled the exchange and Jack's flask bounced valleywards, to be retrieved intact after a few strong words. As we stood to resume the walk a playful gust whisked Alan's cap from his head. It described a graceful arc and eventually came to rest more than half-way towards Stonycroft Gill, amid a small group of unconcerned sheep. There it stayed. If you ever see a Herdwick wearing a flat cap on Causey Pike, don't be surprised!

8

THE PORTALS OF WASDALE
(Some Memories of a Favourite Valley)

There was no moon. We had driven many a mile to reach our valley and now we had arrived there was nothing to see but a thin ribbon of tarmac in the headlights and its fringe of bracken and grass, and an occasional curve in the winding road allowed us to light the lake for a fleeting moment. A sensation of being enclosed by massive mountain shapes grew upon us but it was all in the mind. Our world was bounded by the limits of the headlamp beams, but when we emerged at our journey's end a faint glow penetrated the thin clouds and the sounds of the hills at night surrounded us. It was a long-awaited moment, this introduction to Wasdale, but it was almost like a home-coming. Here we were in the midst of hills as yet unseen, but made familiar by close attention to mountain literature. Until the morning they could remain as portraits of the imagination, aided and abetted by count-less photographs, famous mountains, many of them with names known to folk who would never dream of setting foot on them—Scafell, Scafell Pike, Great Gable, Pillar and Steeple—but on the morrow they would be there to see for the first time, and we would be climbing upon them from Wasdale Head, the traditional home of English mountaineering.

In the 1960s we used to make a point of spending a few days at Wasdale Head every October so that we could enjoy the circle of fells at a time of relative peace. In the process we began to forget that this could be a busy centre, although as recently as then the valley never filled up as it can do nowadays on a busy Bank Holiday weekend. Time and again our little group contrived to be blessed with the best of Lakeland weather as we wandered at will, and as often as not with the hills to ourselves once we moved away from the popular tops and tracks. They were glorious days, followed by pleasant evenings at a famous climbers' inn, and always it seemed that we could never have too much of a good thing. The idea of the night ascent was by no means unknown. How we found the energy remains a mystery.

I remember setting off one midnight for a walk down the valley—no problems of route finding, just follow the road until I felt like turning back. My companions had declined to accompany me so I went alone. The moon was full and cast so much light that I could pick out features on the fellsides far above, the white runnels of tumbling becks, the dark shadows of the crags and a clear-cut mountain skyline that ringed the valley all round. A tracery of cirrus veiled the highest stratosphere with the moon sitting in heavenly splendour, wrapped in this shawl of blue-tinged lace. The only sound was water—the tinkle of the becks turning in their stony beds, the hiss of wavelets rippling along a pebbly Wastwater beach. I walked till the road turned away from the lake, then turned regretfully to face the valley head, not regretting the long road back but regretting that this could not go on for ever. My pace became even slower as I sought to draw out each succeeding moment.

There was a magic here that must be prolonged. It could not last for ever but the end came soon enough—much sooner than expected. From far away came the sound of voices singing, a chorus that excelled in gusto if not in harmony. The spell was broken. My friends, showing commendable concern for my safety, had set out as a self-appointed search party but when we met, a good twenty minutes after their presence had been announced in song, recriminations flowed freely. I could not help thinking that their expressions of anxiety about my well-being were hardly borne out by the joviality of their approach.

Wasdale is largely associated with the mountain giants of England and even the smallest fells in the dale have an air of impregnability about them, rising as they do so abruptly from the level strath that they seem much higher than they really are. There is hardly a hill in the valley that can be recommended as an easy stroll. The fells that guard the entrance to the dale are absolutely typical of the stark, dramatic quality of one of the district's wildest dales.

On one side you see The Screes, and facing from across the way is Buckbarrow, a smaller version of The Screes that stands well back from the lake as though diffident about any resemblance. But there is no diffidence about Buckbarrow if you choose to make a frontal assault. From the road to the summit is a climb of about a thousand feet and if you take it direct you face some of the roughest ground in Lakeland. Of course you can go round the crags but this is hardly playing the game fairly. The crags are Buckbarrow—or Buckbarrow is the crags. Neither *sounds* quite right but the statement conveys the truth of the matter. There is an impressively cairned mound a few hundred yards back from the brink of the cliffs but that is Glade How, higher perhaps, but it has nothing in common with Buckbarrow. The surroundings of Glade How are grass. Buckbarrow is uncompromisingly rock.

When I climbed Buckbarrow—alone—I had no intention of making a flanking movement on either side for that would mean a grassy ascent quite out of keeping with the true nature of the fell. The most obvious rocky gully seemed a likely possibility and, excepting the roughness that goes hand in glove with rarely trodden scree, there were no real problems. It was like a miniature edition of the Great Stone Shoot of Sgurr Alisdair, the highest peak of the Cuillin ridge of the Isle of Skye—with this difference: the Great Stone Shoot is becoming eroded by the passage of countless boots each year, whereas the little stone shoot of Buckbarrow is in an almost virgin state. This situation can make the going tricky. Many of the boulders are precariously balanced but by keeping to the right-hand side—facing in—I had a reasonably secure footing. Here is a little bit of Lakeland which can still give a sensation of the pioneering spirit and in 1965 there was a feeling, probably false, that I was treading where no one had gone before.

Buckbarrow gives an unusual view of a famous valley. The lake is seen in full and The Screes can be studied in detail. Best of all is the Scafell group with its impressive build-up from the valley head. The other side of Buckbarrow is a disappointment, an extensive grassy rise culminating in Seatallan which hides some of the loneliest fell country to be found anywhere in Cumbria, the wide sheep pastures of the Copeland Forest where you can walk for miles and never see a soul. I left Buckbarrow in the direction of Glade How, then turned north-east to visit Greendale Tarn. A group of tiny tents showed that the lads of the Eskdale Outward Bound Centre were settling in for the night. I left them to their pleasures and turned down Greendale Gill to find my car in Wasdale and seek more comfortable repose.

This side of the valley has two more fells which may reasonably be described as minors in the context of the Wasdale fells, Middle Fell and Yewbarrow. They make few concessions to casual walkers, however, and Yewbarrow in particular is a gem of a mountain in miniature that would hold its own in any company. It is the logical conclusion of one of the finest mountain traverses in the land, the Mosedale Horseshoe, a round in the classic tradition if ever there was one. We always called it the Pillar Round in fact, probably because we left out Kirk Fell which is an essential component of the Mosedale Horseshoe proper. On the other hand we did like to include Yewbarrow, which many walkers omit, probably considering that they have done enough when they reach Dore Head where the option is open to take advantage of a steep and quick descent into Mosedale. We have reached the Wastwater Hotel in twenty minutes from the top of Dore Head, but it seems a pity to leave out Yewbarrow even though it is really outside the side valley of Mosedale.

Strangely we never did the Pillar Round in a clockwise direction, not in those early days when our autumn visits were a regular and eagerly awaited event, nor since, for the early habits seem to die hard. I suppose there is no reason against this and no doubt I'll try it some day, but it is certainly easier to make your way round the ridge with the gentle gradient of Black Sail Pass at the outset than to start the climb anywhere else. Yet the real reason for doing the Pillar Round as an anti-clockwise circuit has nothing to do with ease of ascent. To do the Pillar Round— if it is to deserve its name—you must tread the summit of Pillar Mountain and the best walker's approach is by the High Level Traverse to Robinson's Cairn with its continuation up the ridge behind Pillar Rock to the mountain's summit. This is all anticlimax if you go the other way.

When we did start from Yewbarrow we never reached Pillar, but then Yewbarrow is quite worth an ascent for its own sake. A couple of us once set off up Bell Rib on one of those gloriously hot days that are representative of July at its best. It was not all plain sailing but once certain initial problems were put behind us we enjoyed a lazy interlude in the hills that remains a landmark in my mountain memories.

Our tent was pitched beside Wastwater—a practice that would be frowned upon nowadays—and wills that weakened in the summer heat rebelled at the idea of a long mountain walk. We were lounging about in swimming trunks and on the spur of the moment decided to climb the nearest fell. We pulled on our boots but when I slipped a shirt over my shoulders my friend scoffed at the idea and chose to risk the rays of the sun—a decision he had cause to regret soon enough. He developed a lobster complexion which radiated a garish call to attention that would have looked well on a neon advertising sign in Piccadilly Circus. The moral is obvious enough but too often learned the hard way: take the sun in easy stages. Walking stripped to the waist is a pleasure indeed when our climate allows it, but never with pallid flesh that has had half a year to forget the weathering of a previous season.

This was the one and only occasion when I climbed a fell wearing swimming trunks. I suppose it is hardly an example of good practice to others but if called upon to defend our actions we would have said that we only intended to scramble to the top of Yewbarrow and we would be back in half an hour or so. In fact we crossed to Low Tarn—cool and inviting, and for that we were perfectly

Wastwater from Yewbarrow

The rocky summit cone of Bessyboot

Tarn at Leaves, Rosthwaite Fell, with Pike of Stickle in the distance

Wastwater's crags and screes towards the southern end of the lake

Side Pike is the dominating feature of Lingmoor Fell when viewed from the upper reaches of Great Langdale

The southern slopes of Holme Fell in winter

Wintry track to Naddle Fell, St John's in the Vale

Stickle Pike, Dunnerdale, as seen from Tarn Hill

Eagle Crag, Stonethwaite, Borrowdale, casting its shadow over
Greenup Gill

Barf from the southern edge of Bassenthwaite Lake

The summit rocks of Helm Crag

attired. There followed a scramble down Over Beck, more in than out of it, and so back to camp with ravenous appetites. A glorious day for the pair of us. My companion's agonies were yet to come.

There was one incident on Yewbarrow, however, that highlights the character of the fell. Both ends of the ridge are defended by crags. An approach from Dore Head involves a simple scramble up Stirrup Crag. No problems there for anyone of average agility, but the southern end of the ridge is a different proposition altogether. Bell Rib is better left to those who know how to handle themselves on rock, but it can be avoided by using a gully on the left.

This was the end of Yewbarrow that we attacked on that sunny day many years ago, but whereas I was satisfied to acknowledge my limitations my friend chose the frontal assault and bade me farewell with the promise to "See you on top!" I arrived at Great Door and sat on a rock to wait but as time passed there was no sign of him joining me. Thinking that perhaps he had got there ahead of me and gone on I strolled along the ridge to the summit, half a mile or so beyond Great Door. The place was deserted. It was time to start worrying so I hurried back. Still there was no one about. Fearing the worst I scrambled down the gully to search the rocks at the foot of Bell Rib. Nothing. No body, and no reply to my calls. Well, he could have taken much longer than I had allowed so, more in hope than expectation, I turned to the gully once more intending to try a few shouts from the top. I met him at Great Door, returning in all haste from the summit. Apparently he had emerged from the excitements of Bell Rib during my search for his mortal remains below and had duplicated my actions of half an hour earlier. There is a moral here somewhere for those who wish to find it. The only comment that I wish to make is that after our immediate and mutual relief at the sight of each other there followed a series of equally mutual recriminations at each other's thoughtlessness.

Yewbarrow marks the point where the grand group of fells that is Wasdale Head begins and where the introductory fells end. But at the far side of the lake is a mountainside that is as much a part of the essential

Wasdale scene as any of the giants that close the dale: The
Screes. You cannot know Wasdale if you do not know The
Screes. It is impossible to enter the valley and be unaware
of the vast sweep of crumbling crag and scree that tumbles
into the waters of Wastwater itself. The fellside is like a
huge, petrified Niagara, but bigger by far than North
America's most famous waterfall and in autumn the dying
brackens seem to set the patterned fans of debris alight
when lit by the rays of the setting sun.

When I first visited my favourite valley I was amazed to
learn that you can walk along that far shore, but it does
not need keen eyesight to detect the track once you trouble
to look for it. Horrifying tales of overwhelming difficulties
did nothing but encourage us to explore as soon as possible
and we found that, apart from two or three hundred yards
of awkward boulders near the foot of the lake, the way is
relatively simple and straightforward.

On our first visit we encountered our greatest difficulties before setting foot on The Screes at all. Blithely
rejecting the aid of our map we plunged innocently
through thickets at the foot of the lake to find barring our
way a much wider and deeper River Irt than we had
anticipated. The answer to our problem lay in the map
pocket of my anorak, but our brains must have been particularly dull that evening. At the end of a chill October
the four of us decided to wade the icy water so recently released from what must be England's coldest lake.
The crossing, though cold, seemed simple enough—at
first. The trouble was that the greatest depth lay at the far
side so that initial hilarity gradually gave way to
apprehension as unbelievably wintry waves curled higher
and higher, freezing fingers that sought out the more
delicate portions of our anatomy. In the circumstances
perhaps the remark that the "Irt" was considerable could
be forgiven. On the far bank we stamped vigorously up and
down to restore a reluctant circulation and dug out the
map. There must be a better way of doing it than this!
There was. The bridge was barely a hundred yards down-
stream. Fortunately there were no ladies present. . . .

A new path has been opened since then, leading from a

stile near the cattle grid where the road reaches the lake. This footway—compliments of the National Trust—completes an attractive outing of about nine miles. The circuit of Wastwater includes a considerable section along the Wasdale road. To a walker of the fells the very idea of treading a metalled highway is abhorrent, but here is an exception that can be justified if you do this part first. By starting at the head of the lake you can survey the complete route along The Screes from the unobstructed viewpoint of the road, rather like studying a map before setting out on a journey, and it is interesting to compare the reality, when you reach it, with any preconceived notions that may have been formed. And when you do set foot on The Screes you are facing up-valley which is the best way to be, so that you have the justly famous mountain group around Wasdale Head, the National Park symbol, in front of you all the way—although you will not be much aware of it in that first three hundred yards!

This is not the only walk that involves The Screes. You are apt to forget, as you stare at that wide-screen display across England's deepest lake, that the plunging waste of decaying stone is only a front. There is another side and a summit. Two summits in fact, high points at either end of a wide ridge. Whin Rigg is nearer the entrance to the valley, and rather more than a mile along the ridge is the higher Illgill Head. These are the real names of the mountain that most of us call The Screes. In the depression between them are two small tarns, small enough to feel the pinch in times of drought. An alternative to the circuit of Wastwater, and a very satisfying alternative too, is to combine the scree track with a traverse of the ridge.

A couple of us once tackled this walk when the peaceful air in the valley was contradicted by one of Lakeland's fiercest gales on the ridge. It is worth commenting that you should never judge conditions on the tops by reference to what you experience below. Weather in mountain country is subject to variation far more than anyone with only lowland experience can ever realize. Different altitudes can mean different weather and even good weather on the tops can change with startling rapidity, as many an unprepared walker will testify. Failure to take account of these extremes may well have fatal results, so be prepared. I suppose most of us tend to take unwarranted chances at times and often we get away with it, but if you meet with the worst before accumulating the experience to deal with it the consequences have a fair chance of being tragic.

When we walked over Illgill Head and Whin Rigg in a furious gale we were dressed as we should be—no bathing costumed frolic, this. We dared not venture near the escarpment, magnificent though the downward prospect is, and our caution was well taken. I remember being lifted bodily into the air and carried forward several yards, legs spinning wildly like a character in a Styx cartoon. The most unnerving part of this experience was being set down the right way up, able to continue walking as though nothing had happened. As the wind increased we made progress on all fours but later, beside the lake again, there was only a playful breeze to remind us of the turmoil aloft. That was one of the most violent winds I have known, a great experience—especially in retrospect, though not always pleasant at the time.

The southern flank of the ridge is as placid and uneventful as the other side is dramatic, a gentle slope of turf becoming wet and boggy away from the watershed, which suggests nothing of interest below. For those who demand bold and aggressive scenery this is true. The valley of Miterdale is pastoral for half its length then, narrowing, leads directly to Burnmoor Tarn with Scafell beyond. Surprisingly, the River Mite does not rise in Burnmoor Tarn but on the slopes of Illgill Head.

Some of my happiest days in Lakeland have been spent in and around Wasdale. For the most part they have been strenuous days, walking to some purpose with companions whose feelings have been in tune with my own. Sarah has not been there yet, but before long she will be leading me a dance around the Wasdale fells. I hope I'll be up to it.

9

INTERESTING CORNERS

(Lingmoor Fell; Blea Rigg; Naddle Fell; Holme Fell)

Great height is no guarantee of quality when judging the respective merits of the fells of Lakeland. Some of the highest hills may be smooth grassy mounds on which you can see most of what there is to be seen by taking a simple walk over the summit. Others of quite modest altitude compensate for their lack of stature by having an immense wealth of character. Loughrigg, Silver How and Grange Fell, all barely above the thousand-foot mark, make a trio quite typical of this category and the supreme example—Haystacks—is less than 2,000 feet in height. The fells described in the following pages range from 1,040 feet to 1,776 feet and they are all a pleasure to tread, full of secret little corners, laced with becks and gills, dotted with minor summits and hollows that may contain tiny tarns, and all are a joy to explore.

What is it about these particular little hills that makes them such splendid places for easy-going wanderers who like nothing better than to amble about on modest foot-hills packed with interest? The answer may be summed up in a single word—glaciation. At the height of the last ice age the valley glaciers would rise above the level of the lower intervening ridges and cross them with a scouring action. The more resistant volcanic rocks would defy the ice sufficiently to produce the ruggedly uneven terrain known to the expert as a mammilated topography. After the ice came the return of vegetation and many of the smaller hills have their pockets of woodland, much quite recent. Man would make his mark—most obviously in mining and quarrying activities—so that we have a wide selection of minor fells where you can potter around all day if you wish, not covering much ground perhaps, but always finding something of interest in these special corners of the fells.

LINGMOOR FELL

Strangely, for a hill with so much to offer and so close to a fell-walking base as popular as Ambleside, Lingmoor is relatively neglected. Its misfortune is in being situated near the mouth of a valley abounding in attractions for walkers, and if you do look for a small hill for the odd off-day you have both Loughrigg and Wansfell on Ambleside's doorstep, much nearer than Lingmoor, so that you can step on to them directly from the streets of the little tourist-oriented town. If you do choose to follow the Langdale road, then Bowfell, Crinkle Crags, Pike o' Blisco and the famous Langdale Pikes exert a stronger attraction. Lingmoor is at the wrong side of the valley, too, with the moat of Great Langdale Beck between the road and the fell so it is hardly surprising that it is so often passed by when the fells of the valley head are framed in your windscreen.

Perhaps there is a tendency to regard Lingmoor as a forgotten fell, but though this is not strictly true fellow visitors do tend to be thin on the ground. You can relax on the summit even in the height of summer and expect to enjoy a spell of peace and quiet, and as you do so it is worth bearing in mind that you are on a sort of traffic island, surrounded on all sides by throngs of humanity. Cars often choke the roads that bound the fell, in Great Langdale to the north and east, Little Langdale to the south and the Blea Tarn road which connects the two valleys round the west of the fell.

The Blea Tarn road makes use of a depression sliced through the southern wall of Great Langdale by an overflow distributory of the main Langdale glacier as it escaped into Little Langdale, its path eased by a zone of weaker rock following the line of Mickleden across the ridge. The tarn occupies a hollow scooped out by the action of ice. Blea Tarn is the one feature that brings visitors to Lingmoor, though it is fair to say that not one in a thousand of the motorists who pause to view the water knows the name of the fell on which he has parked his car. These sightseers may stroll down to the shore and maybe visit the rhododendrons on the other side, perhaps they may even know that this ground is described by Wordsworth in *The Excursion* (Book II) and that Bleatarn House between the tarn and the head of the little pass was his Abode of the Solitary, but Lingmoor remains a closed book.

Wordsworth described the panorama seen from Lingmoor, though what he would think if he were to come down to the tarn and find the place as it is now on a warm day in summer can only be imagined—no suitable abode for any Solitary, to be sure! But then, Wordsworth was the district's first major publicity agent so he could have no real cause for complaint. If only he had known what he was starting.

The Blea Tarn gap is a good side for an ascent of Lingmoor because of the excellent views of the Langdale Pikes, with pleasing foregrounds of trees or rock. Ascents from the Langdale valley, at Elterwater or Chapel Stile, can result in complications caused by quarries. There is a great deal of tree cover on this side too and access is somewhat restricted because the beck comes between the fell and the road. This side of the fell is really better to look at than to climb. Indeed it is a most attractive aspect, if you can tear your eyes away from the Langdale Pikes. When we drive up the dale I always find myself waiting for the moment when Side Pike springs into view. This thumb of rock is only half the height of those famous Pikes across the way but it manages to convey the same visual impact as its better-known cousins. Side Pike almost demands to be climbed. "We'll do it, one day," we always said as it came into view. It was a long time before we converted ambition into action but the event was well worth the waiting.

Side Pike comes as near to being inaccessible as almost any top in Lakeland, apart from Pillar Rock—which anyway is purely a rock-climbers' preserve. Side Pike is only practicable for the walker on one side. Though connected to the main fell by a well-defined ridge there is no possibility of an ascent from that side. You have to bypass it and approach from the west.

Fortunately there is no need to lose height in doing this. Although at first glance it seems necessary to descend almost to the foot of the ridge to get past, close inspection reveals a rake on the south side. A large, detached block appears to bar access to the rake but it conceals a "fat man's agony" of a gap that brings you out on an airy ledge. For those whose girth lends uncertainty to the procedure there is an alternative on the lower side of the block, where a simple scramble involving a stout heave on a well-placed handhold is all that is needed to reach the same ledge. With Sarah riding "papoose" I found the latter course necessary and the fact that I was happy enough to make the move in these circumstances is sure evidence of the simplicity and safety of the manoeuvre.

The shelf is wide enough to provide a satisfying sense of security, yet sufficiently exposed to give a short and exhilarating traverse across Side Pike's craggy southern face. There is a spectacular view of Blea Tarn resting like a pool in a saucer below your feet, and one's ego enjoys a pleasant boost at the sight of those cars crawling along the ribbon of road down there. Most of those travellers will be marvelling in genuine enough appreciation at the scenery as they see it, but imagine their feelings were they to be transported to your viewpoint. It is only 300 feet above and perhaps a quarter of a mile distant, but a world away in terms of physical experience. They cannot know the joys that you—and all fell walkers—enjoy, yet with a minimum of effort and a modicum of fellcraft, or someone to guide them, all but the infirm could reach this point and understand something of the force that motivates men to walk the fells. The tiny traverse, a miniature Jack's Rake, all too soon contours the crag and before you know it gives way to broken ground and joins the track coming up from the W. H. Brown memorial seat at Blea Tarn Pass. It is one of the prizes of Lingmoor, the sort of place that calls for an action replay. Certainly, on my first visit I went back to do it again.

Another prize of this little fell is Lingmoor Tarn. Though only a small and shallow pool nestling with its scatter of overgrown islands in a peaty hollow, this is a tarn in the best Lakeland tradition. In the right season there is a magical quality about the spot. On a sunny afternoon in June the backing of tumbling heather broken by sunlit outcrops running up to the summit makes a delightful surround to placid ripples on water bespeckled with flecks of white where lilies and the dainty bogbean flourish. Approach along the short undulating track from the top of the fell and you see a splendid foreground that shows the rugged skyline of the Pikes across Langdale to great advantage.

Lingmoor has a part claim on a third tarn for the southern flank below Bush Pike reaches down to Little Langdale Tarn which, with the young River Brathay, marks the limits of the fell in that direction. Wandering in Little Langdale we found an exuberant display of Policeman's Helmet overflowing a damp hollow by the road. This is the popular name for the Himalayan Balsam, an imported flower that is now widespread in Britain. Together with the famous Blea Tarn rhododendrons its presence gives this low-lying fell an unlikely link with the highest mountains in the world.

Lingmoor is a fell that has something for everyone; young or old, timid or adventurous—even the rock climber can find minor crags on which to test his skills if only he can tear himself away from the better-known climbing grounds at the head of Langdale. Lingmoor even has a "needle", though the Oak Howe pinnacle is somewhat blunter than its famous counterpart on the Napes ridges of Great Gable. So spare a thought for little Lingmoor when the popular fells are overcrowded. You won't regret your choice.

BLEA RIGG

We met him on the summit of Silver How, one of those cheerful extroverts who is never short of a spot of quick repartee. We were enjoying the prospect of Grasmere's pleasant acres when he arrived, red and perspiring but with a grin as wide as the Wasdale Screes splitting his face. We asked him if he had enjoyed the climb.

"Splendid, splendid!" he beamed. "But I think I'll go down a different way. You should never go down a mountain the same way that you come up, you know!" He gazed at our reclining figures, his eyebrows raised in an expression of apparently innocent inquiry. The trap was sprung and I stepped right in.

"Really? Why?"

"Well, you *do* come up head first, don't you?"

After that our sojourn on Silver How could only come to an end. He was a pleasant and friendly enough fellow but the spell was broken. After a little more banter we went on our way. We did take his advice, however, and leave the fell in a different direction, north-west along the ridge of Blea Rigg.

This fell might be described as the south-east ridge of High Raise and its natural termination is one of the finest of all the little fells of Lakeland, Loughrigg. Logically, ascents should start there, on the slope overlooking Ambleside, if the ridge is to be followed in its entirety. The connection with Silver How is made at the col of Red Bank and if the thing is done properly both Blea Rigg and Sergeant Man will be traversed to reach one of the most central heights in the Lake District. On the day in question Blea Rigg was the limit of our explorations, with a return by Easedale to Grasmere. The walking is pleasant but the terrain is far too widespread to give much sensation of ridge-walking, though the name of this wedge of high land is in accord with such a description. After all, "rigg" is an old north-country name for a ridge.

"Blea" is derived from the Old Norse for dark, or blue. Dark is hardly an adjective that readily springs to mind when describing Blea Rigg for this land is open to the sky, a place for gentle summer wanderings with a light heart and a springy step. On the other hand, the northern flank has an impressive wall of rock, Blea Crag by name. It faces away from the sun and is generally in shadow so "dark" would be an adequate description. It could be that the name of the fell has its origins in views from this direction.

Whatever the source of the name, Blea Rigg is well worth a
visit. Like so much of the fell country in the neighbourhood it is a hill of many summits, without any really
distinctive top. The usually recognized summit is at 1,776
feet, but it is certainly not the highest point since the ridge
continues to rise as you progress towards the west and for
this reason is easy to miss. It is reasonable to expect lower
ground to surround the summit of any hill.

There are plenty of other eminences, many of which
deserve to be sought out, and the undulating ground is full
of unsuspected hollows, some containing cheerful pools of
quiet water. The largest seems to be Lang Howe Tarn. It
has a number of alternative names, all of them quite
justifiable, but as Lang Howe is a nearby knoll Lang Howe
Tarn is good enough for me. As you approach from Silver
How you come upon it suddenly as you round a small
upthrust of land and its placid, reedy surface forms an
excellent foreground to the distant excitement of the
Langdale Pikes—as many a photographer will testify. The
tarn is quite shallow and tends to become overgrown in
summer but if the weather is right all this lends a certain
charm to the scene.

Lang Howe Tarn may be the largest on the fell but there
are two much more considerable stretches of water that
help to define its limits. One is Stickle Tarn, but this has
such an affinity for the Langdale Pikes that it is almost
heresy to think of it in connection with Blea Rigg. The
other is Easedale Tarn. There is a link with another fell
here too—Tarn Crag is named after it, of course—but Blea
Rigg seems justified in making at least an equal claim.
Perhaps Blea Rigg is rarely in the minds of those who visit
or pass Easedale Tarn but the summit is only half a mile
away. The tarn itself is about a quarter of a mile long and
there is evidence of another one-time tarn on a step higher
up the valley. The Easedale track has a reputation for
being one of the wettest popular paths in Lakeland.

The large, untidy cairn piled against a huge boulder
near the foot of the tarn has a history unsuspected by
anyone new to Easedale. These stones are the last remnants of a hut that once stood on the site. It was built about

a century ago as a shelter for visitors who rode up to the tarn on ponies, but it later became a refreshment hut and no doubt did a roaring trade on hot summer afternoons. The proprietor, Mr William Wilson of Goody Bridge, would carry up his supplies in panniers on a donkey and the bottles of mineral waters were stored in a hole under the floor for coolness—no ice or refrigeration in those days. The large boulder was a cornerstone of the hut and jutted into the interior. An old faded photograph I was shown indicated traces of cultivation in the shape of a little flower bed along the front of the hut. Mr Wilson's son and family carried on the enterprise between the wars but after the last war the little building gradually deteriorated. In the 1960s the process of decay accelerated rapidly so that it is now a sort of modern-day tumulus; a memorial to more leisurely times when a visit to Easedale Tarn was a great adventure and the pilgrimage to the summits was left to a discriminating—and some thought eccentric—minority.

Blea Rigg shapes the valley's northern flank between the Langdale Pikes and Chapel Stile, a general area occasionally known as Langdale Fell. The most direct ascent on this side is by way of White Gill where it is possible to watch the antics of rock climbers on Whitegill Crag, Blea Rigg's major cragsman's playground. Beyond the excitements of the rock scenery in the ravine the ascent is relatively dull and the actual whereabouts of the summit is open to doubt on a skyline with a number of tops, some of which seem obviously higher than the one usually accepted. Alternatively, a start can be made from Dungeon Ghyll New Hotel. This enables the summit to be approached along the ridge from the west and provides the walker with the peculiar sensation of *descending* to the summit!

This route can involve a pleasant little scramble. You cross to the true left (east) bank of Mill Gill and look for a diversion across the lower ramparts of Tarn Crag (not to be confused with Easedale's Tarn Crag). The rake is safe enough to walk up without the use of hands—given a reasonable sense of balance—and gives a touch of gentle excitement for those who like to come to grips with rock in relatively safe situations.

Blea Rigg is a pleasant expanse of fell with much of the character of its personal foothills, Loughrigg and Silver How. To follow the ridge is a rewarding experience with fine views, often framed by an interesting foreground of rocky or grassy knolls. It is a walk best done from east to west so that the challenging outline of the Langdale Pikes is for ever appearing and reappearing ahead, an excellent approach to that splendid group. But Blea Rigg is quite worth a visit in its own right. If you have not done it yet, do try it some time.

NADDLE FELL

As you drive from Dunmail Raise towards Keswick nothing seems more certain than the fact that you will follow a major valley all the way. When you reach Causeway Foot and begin the short climb over the ridge of Castlerigg the illusion is spoilt, yet this is merely a short-cut across the watershed to Derwentwater on the other side. But the facts are not all as they appear. The trouble is that roads impose a false geography on the shape of the land, especially as seen on a map. There is no guarantee that you will see the topography of an area as it should be because the brightly coloured major roads draw attention to themselves and overrule the truth of the contours.

The outflow from Thirlmere tells no lies. It switches its line to the east and flows under the A591 at Smaithwaite Bridge to cut a narrow valley round the eastern flank of Naddle Fell. Two watersheds are crossed by the A591 between Dunmail Raise and Keswick, the first between St John's Beck and Naddle Beck, the second at Castlerigg. It matters little to the motorist and is of small consequence geographically. These are minor watersheds and by the time you reach Keswick the waters of St John's and Naddle Becks are together again in the River Greta.

Naddle Fell is rather like an island, moated by green valleys. At points along the lakeside road—when you can get a view over the trees—it would seem that the hill blocks the valley completely, which just does not make sense. You have just come over a pass so the water must escape somewhere else. Manchester may be thirsty but the city does not take it all and, anyway, a century ago Manchester took none. Yet I believe that most strangers get the answer wrong as they drive west of Naddle Fell on their way to Keswick.

You go below the level of Thirlmere soon after passing the King's Head Inn at Thirlspot and by the time Smaithwaite Bridge is reached the water level is some fifty feet above your head. There follows a barely perceptible climb of about sixty feet which takes you into the Naddle valley. This is the watershed, slight though it may be, that connects Naddle Fell with the fells of central Lakeland. It is the only connection that this small ridge has with any other high country for really and truly Naddle Fell comes as close to being a complete individual as any hill in the Lake District.

You can get almost as much pleasure walking round the fell as you can by climbing it. The Vale of St John's is a delightful, quiet place, and the Naddle valley is more than ordinarily pleasant despite its trunk road. Connect the two valleys by the little pass that contains the Church of St John's-in-the-Vale—built at this point to serve the two valleys—and you have a trip easy enough to satisfy the most lethargic of pedestrians. We used to go this way in the early sixties from a Keswick base and with never a thought of climbing to the top of the fell. Our first port of call would be the stone circle at Castlerigg, then down to Dale Bottom and over the pass into the Vale of St John's. This has long been a regular routine for many a holiday maker staying in the Keswick area, though too many of them do it by car. Our continuation led to the narrowing of the dale, then across the main road at Smaithwaite Bridge, through plantations—we always managed to choose an inordinately wet route—back to Dale Bottom and through pastures to the Brockle Beck route into Keswick.

It is a while since we went that way but I remember with affection the short section of the Vale of St John's where the path turns up the flank of Naddle Fell and allowed us

to file between trees below Wren Crag, with St John's Beck
glistening through leaves, steeply below. Not many trees,
as I remember it, and the track did not hug the steep
fellside for very long. In fact, we knew that when those
trees were reached and the track made its short climb,
then in a minute or two—unless we took our time, as we
usually did—we would be round the corner and approaching Smaithwaite Bridge.

This little corner between the A591 and Low Bridgend,
where the valley narrows so much that it can almost be
called a gorge, has always seemed to hold a spell of its own,
an indescribable something that makes it special. Perhaps
that is why Arthurian legend that has been linked with
the spot has a plausible ring about it. With Wren Crag on
one side, the Castle Rock of Triermain on the other, and
the tree-clad pyramid of Great How closing the gorge at its
head, the place seems to be touched by the sort of romance
of which legends are made. I know of not a single historical
fact that can be used to lend credence to a vague tradition
of Sir Gawain having met the Green Knight here. It is a
pity. When wreaths of mist cling to the steeply pitched
sweep of fell behind Castle Rock and wisps of white vapour
weave patterns in the tall conifers of Great How there is a
sense of mystery about the place that makes one wish—
almost believe—the tradition to be true, and as you turn
an unexpected corner it would be no surprise to find the
Green Chapel still there, having stood undiscovered since
the days of legend.

The best walk is a traverse of the whole fell, south to
north, so that you have the magnificent mountain wall of
Blencathra in front of you the whole time, and you finish
with it mirrored in Tewet Tarn at the end of the day. That's
the way we went when Naddle Fell eventually drew us to
its summit in the early seventies. If you leave a car parked
at the northern end you can combine the route with a
pleasant stroll through the Vale of St John's and enjoy the
little wooded traverse beneath Wren Crag before returning along the ridge. You will still have plenty of time to
sample the delights of the southern half of Naddle Fell at
leisure and find places with fascinating names like

Cowrake Head, Paper Moss and the springheads of William's Beck as you go.

The summit cairn is situated on a little table of rock protruding above the grass, not much higher than a few other likely spots nearby but sufficiently distinctive to be unmistakable. The view is interesting without being outstanding for, with so much higher ground on all sides, it is of necessity restricted. The longest view is to the west across the lowest part of the hills of central Lakeland where the land falls to the north of Bleaberry Fell. You can see the heights of Red Pike and Starling Dodd at the far side of Buttermere, with the abrupt point of Catbells a good direction indicator to help in identification. Pride of place must go to Blencathra. The ridges and gullies of that impressive south face are seen to great advantage from this modest height. Clough Head looks quite good too, which is an unusual compliment for Clough Head always appears to me as a particularly uninteresting sort of fell from most viewpoints and no one of my acquaintance has anything flattering to say about it.

The little ridge that almost seals Thirlmere within its afforested valley may be low, small in area perhaps, but it is certainly not lacking in interest. You can do worse—much worse—than spend a few hours on and about Naddle Fell.

HOLME FELL
There are some localities of no great size, which make little show on the map, yet provide outstandingly attractive contributions to the Lake District scene. A prime example of this is the triangle of countryside bounded by Little Langdale, the A593 road between Skelwith Bridge and Coniston, and the Tilberthwaite valley east of Wetherlam. The most elevated ground within these boundaries is the top of Holme Fell, not much over a thousand feet in height but the focal point of a truly fascinating area. It is not a summit recognized individually on O.S. maps, which show the highest measured point as Ivy Crag at 995 feet. However, west of Ivy Crag there is a contour at 1,025 feet on the 2½-inch map and the

crest of the fell is certainly in excess of this. But height is not everything; if Holme Fell failed to reach the four-figure standard it would still find a place here, on merit, because it has so much to offer that should put it securely on any walker's itinerary.

The fiercest aspect of this little fell is presented to travellers moving north from Coniston along the A593. Here, where the small but beautiful valley of Yewdale Beck reaches back to Tilberthwaite, is a façade of cliffs with the pinnacle of Raven Crag threatening the entry to the little side-dale. Two minor roads pass below Raven Crag, separated by the waters of Yewdale Beck. One leads to Tilberthwaite, the other takes you through the tiny hamlet of Holme Ground on the way to Hodge Close quarries.

Some of the excavations on Holme Fell and the adjoining territory are impressively deep and the heaps of spoil are extensive. If the area was to be stripped of its tree-cover the resemblance to a crater-pocked lunar landscape would surely be undeniable. Holme Fell's most spectacular workings are at Hodge Close. To come unawares on the two great quarries is a particularly vertiginous sensation. These tremendous artificial holes have come very close to unity. An archway has been carved to grant access from one to the other, so we may consider them as Siamese twins, of a kind.

There was a time when an ingeniously efficient gravity railway was used to lift slate from the depths. A laden truck was connected to an empty partner by a cable which was passed round a pulley at the head of the incline. The empty truck was filled with water until it outweighed the lower vehicle and pulled it to the top. When unloading was completed the water-laden twin was drained and in its turn hauled up by water power. This system has been used with profit elsewhere—at Goathland in the North Yorkshire Moors, for example—but at Hodge Close there was an insurmountable drawback. The water accumulating in the quarry had no escape and a more conventional means of raising the slate had to be found. The southern quarry still has its artificial lake.

The water supply for the mineral railway came from a

reservoir on the fell. In fact, all of Holme Fell's tarns are
man-made. There is a shallow, tree-girt pool near the
largest quarry and others some 500 yards to the south,
about half-way between Hodge Close and the summit of
the fell. One has been drained—probably because of a
weakness in the dam—but two remain as decorative addi-
tions to their surroundings. Of the remaining pair the
larger is a place of charm, edged with trees along one bank
and from their shade there is a delightful outlook towards
the highest part of Holme Fell. Autumn is the time to be
there, when the changing leaves on one side complement
the colourful bracken on the other and outcropping rocks
on the summit ridge beyond bring a flavour of the higher
mountains to highlight the scene.

Yew Tree Tarn beside the Ambleside–Coniston road is
another man-made pool, in this case the purpose being to
provide a trout fishery. Poised above it is Ivy Crag, often
assumed to be the highest point until you reach it. Here is
the most conspicuous cairn, a positive magnet to visitors
who must feel a sense of frustration when they get there.
Higher land is not far distant but defended by a rocky gulf
and a wall of crags, a couple of hundred yards away in a
straight line but a round trip of half a mile by way of
Uskdale Gap. This true summit resembles a petrified
ridge tent, torn in tatters by a Lakeland gale. There is a
small cairn on a point of rock with another on a duplicate
outcrop a few yards north. For all its moderate altitude
this is a top of real character, a splendid viewpoint and as
often as not a place of solitude.

The most obvious hills in view are Wetherlam and Coniston's Old Man, which is to be expected since Holme Fell
rests almost in their shadows. Yet the mountains are
upstaged by a lowland prospect. To the south is Coniston
Water and from nowhere else can the extent of this lake
be better appreciated. On the right it laps the moorland
foothills of the Coniston Fells and on the far side of its
waters are the undulations of Grizedale Forest, approximately equivalent in height to this viewpoint. The sombre
greens of pine and fir provide a contrast to brighter colours
elsewhere.

On a visit to Holme Fell on the final weekend of summer in the mid-seventies I climbed to the summit in exceptionally good conditions. After a night of rain the sun shone gently in an atmosphere filled with the tang of imminent autumn. All was sharp and clear. There was a curious impression of magnification about the panorama—rather like viewing through the zoom lens of a movie camera. The hills of south-east Lakeland seemed only a short stroll away with the vale of Troutbeck pointing to the good things of the High Street range. Fairfield and Helvellyn were hardly less dramatic than the Coniston group just over my shoulder. Away to the east the Howgill Fells filled the horizon with a commanding presence, challenging their exclusion from the Lake District National Park. More distant was a south-eastern skyline of the Pennines. A flat-topped silhouette peeping across this far array could only be that giant of the Yorkshire Dales, Ingleborough.

This was an afternoon snatched from the grasp of a workaday world. Not long before it had seemed unlikely that there would be any summit for me that day but as I stood atop little Holme Fell I reflected that the pleasures of this wide display were all the more satisfying because they were unexpected and Scafell Pike would have been hard put to equal Holme Fell on this occasion. There is no need to climb the highest fells to taste the true flavour of the Lakeland hills. The foothill fells of Lingmoor, Blea Rigg, Naddle Fell, Holme Fell and many more are packed with interest and minor excitements and are blessed with breath-taking scenery. They can say it all. Choose the right time and approach them with a sense of personal involvement and they stand comparison with the best in the land.

10

DUDDON INTERLUDE
(Mountain Days in Miniature)

It may be reasonable to suggest that the Duddon valley does not attract fell walkers in quite the same way as most of Lakeland's major valleys, not for any lack of merit, but because it is different. The river follows a sinuous course along a narrow strath, closely hemmed by the valley walls. And there are trees. This is a valley of trees, coniferous plantations round Harter Fell and mile after mile of deciduous and mixed woodland lower down. It is a valley without a lake, though that does not make it unique, but the sound of tumbling water is never far away. This will never be a centre for climbing the larger, more generally popular fells. Of course the Coniston Fells and Crinkle Crags enclose the head of the dale, and Bowfell is not so very far away, but you are at the wrong side of these mountains to see them at their best. Black Combe might be described as a Duddon Fell, but really it is outside the valley, a fell of the coastal plain. Only Harter Fell of the well-known hills has genuine links with the Duddon, and Harter Fell now has its skirt of plantations on this side so that for most folk it is primarily associated with Eskdale.

No, the attractions of this long, winding dale are quite different from those of other large valleys. The Duddon is tucked away on the quieter side of the Lake District, but it reaches right into the heart of the real fell country. When you get up to Cockley Beck Bridge you are on the doorstep of the highest land in England. You can walk up Moasdale to step into the wilderness of upper Eskdale and have the wildest, most worthwhile side of the Scafells at your fingertips—which is a good way of putting it since scrambling is often the order of the day when you approach those giants from this direction. It is a long and, for most folk, an arduous approach to Scafell Pike yet, if your legs will let you do it, one of the best ways of all. But Scafell and its Pike are in no way Duddon fells. This is a valley of foothills and a valley for the connoisseur. For me the real Duddon valley is to be found in the middle and lower reaches where mixed woodlands line the dale and cascades and pools make the Duddon one of the most fascinating rivers in all the fell country. Devotees will tell you that this is the finest valley of them all.

Twenty years ago I came into contact—very briefly— with the land of the Duddon for the first time. We were driving to Wasdale for a few autumn days at Wasdale Head. We came over Wrynose Pass out of Little Langdale and paused at Cockley Beck Bridge to stretch our legs before going on over Hardknott Pass. We stretched our legs more than we had intended. Seven of us, and a considerable weight of food and equipment, shared a couple of cars—an old M.G. Midget and an even more ancient Hillman. The latter found the task beyond its scope with a full load so we sent it ahead with its driver while four of us walked up the pass, playing cards as we went! At the summit we found the M.G. pulled in at the side of the road, bonnet cover raised and issuing clouds of vapour like the pride of La'al Ratty getting up steam for a fast run to the coast. After a sufficient pause during which we discussed strategy we resettled in these chariots to face the descent, not without a certain amount of trepidation.

The M.G. went first. A minute later we passed it, again stationary beside the road, at the bottom of the first vicious hairpin. We stopped as soon as convenient and climbed back to investigate. When we looked into the little sports car it was like looking at a scene from one of those Ealing film comedies that brought the smiles back to Britain's face after the war. "Taff" was still in his driving seat— knee-deep in potatoes. There had been a sack of them behind his head but as he had nosed down the first really steep bank they had cascaded round his ears and bounced round his feet like puffed wheat pouring into a cereal bowl. How he had managed to apply the brake we never did find out.

On our next visit to Wasdale we deemed it wise to eschew the high passes, having regard to the shortcomings of our transport. We chose a route round the coast and into the Duddon valley, and before taking the fell road from Ulpha into Eskdale we broke the journey to sample the hospitality of the old Traveller's Rest at Ulpha. After a short stay we departed from the inn, piled into the car and drove into the dark of night full of youthful enthusiasm. We would have been well advised to study our map in more detail. Though the contours are obscured by trees and packed lettering the symbol denoting a gradient of at least one-in-five is quite explicit. So the car swung innocently round the corner to be confronted by a rearing stretch of tarmac that looked as vertical as Pillar Rock in the head-lights' beam. There was the inevitable stall and we rolled gently back into the car park for a second attempt.

The foregoing has only an incidental connection with fell walking but it serves as an introduction to the roads of the Duddon valley. They are narrow, winding and few; hardly a place for the novice motorist. At the very en-trance to the dale there is a steep bank that can bring palpitations to the hearts of pusillanimous drivers. Yet if you drive with confidence, care and consideration for others the road up the dale, and those leading into it, are a pleasure to follow.

In those earlier days we drove this way with hardly a thought for the Duddon fells. Black Combe, at least, was a name we knew. As a final outpost of the fells in south-east Lakeland it is a hill of some importance but even Black Combe was compelled to bide its time when the great mountains in the heart of the district called our eager, youthful selves. The loss was ours. These hills are gener-ally small but some of them are very prickly, particularly the Dunnerdale Fells to the east of the valley's mouth. The first that we climbed came almost by accident.

There was an October weekend in 1970 when Lakeland put on one of those displays of rainfall for which it is—perhaps unjustly—famous. The road at Wasdale Head was under water. Mosedale Beck had burst its banks near Down-in-the-Dale Bridge but we had arranged to meet friends at the Wastwater Hotel so, with water rippling round the door sills, we drove cautiously forward. This was one day when the collective urge to reach for high places was at a low ebb and a majority decision saw us turn our backs on the waterlogged Wasdale scene. However, the idea of forgoing the fells altogether met with some resistance so we cast around for a small hill that might offer some reward on even this most unlikely day. Our choice was one of the district's shapeliest tiny fells, Stickle Pike. A wet day is not really the best of times to visit this little peak, but at least we did not go home unsatisfied. You cannot begin to know the fell country until you have seen it in all its guises and even the smallest of hills can provide the sort of experience of which memories are made.

Stickle Pike is one of a number of modest hills that thrust skywards to claim an individuality over the lengthy ridge running from the sea to the Coniston Fells. This is the ridge that forms the eastern watershed of the Duddon valley. It climbs in gradual stages to a small 2,000-foot contour ring at Walna Scar, beyond which the Lakeland fells proper are usually considered to begin. Yet though these smaller hills may lack in stature there is no doubt that some of them display the real characteristics of mountain Lakeland—if in miniature. Both Stickle Pike and its neighbour, Caw, are eye-catching peaks on the rough skyline that faces motorists travelling west towards Broughton along the A5092, though Dow Crag and Coniston Old Man are the ones that they can usually put a name to if the names of the fells do readily come to mind. This has always been an exciting road for me, usually a prelude to those weekends at Wasdale Head, with the turn into the Duddon valley a moment to savour.

Stickle Pike and its approaches offer so much in small compass, enough to put many a more massive fell to shame. On that wet and misty day in 1970 we hardly tasted the true flavour of this mini-mountain but through the drifting mists and determined drizzle there filtered a promise of what might be. We left the fell accompanied by a mounting squall to rejoin wives who had prudently sought shelter before the worst of the weather could return. Soon the fells were awash with rain that seemed certain to be with us for the rest of the day—and night.

On a later visit we found the spiky little hill transformed. Here was everything that an easy-going wanderer could wish; pleasant tracks to follow, tarns, streams, waterfalls, small crags and a splendid summit with views of delight, all there for the taking with hardly any test of wind and limb. In the right season, with the right weather, the colours of the fellside flora complete a scene of the highest quality.

Stickle Pike is the craggy pyramid that crowns the highest point of this part of a wandering ridge, its topmost rocks reaching the modest height of 1,231 feet. For practical purposes this crest can be taken as the climax of those Dunnerdale Fells that rise from the northern finger of the Duddon estuary. South of this point are other minor tops. They include Great Stickle where the 1,000-foot contour is first used—or at least it would be if the cartographers were able to squeeze a contour ring round a spot height of 1,001 feet. From the south this appears as a nicely formed little peak and it is a good viewpoint too.

A striking feature in the immediate neighbourhood of Great Stickle is a line of white boulders exposed by a wandering stream a few hundred yards to the south-east. Bathed by the searching rays of beneficial sunshine they remind you of newly white-washed stones in a regimental rockery prior to an inspection by the top brass. Limestone! It appears foreign in what is typical Lakeland country, even if everything is on a miniaturized scale. Yet south-east of the Dunnerdale Fells is a narrow band of calcareous rock stretching far across the southern fringe of the Lake District mountains. It passes between Coniston and its fells and takes its name from there: the Coniston Limestone. Rarely is it seen better than here, beside Great Stickle, like a string of pearls washed to a sparkling freshness by the tumbling waters of Stickletongue and Hare Gill Becks.

Further away a pattern of pastures decorates the gentle hillside that rises beyond the River Lickle. Great Stickle has a good outlook over the sea too. It is a fine spot for enjoying an early lunch after a late—or lazy—start and with your back against convenient rocks you can gaze over the ridge where it descends in fits and starts to the coastal road at Duddon Bridge.

Great Stickle and Stickle Pike—the names on the map are an exciting intimation of all that waits to be discovered. There is even a Little Stickle, and there are knotts, pikes, hows and barrows, all names which have the ring of the real fell country about them. Between Great Stickle and Stickle Pike is a small area that seems at first glance an uninteresting tract of grassy hummocks. The wide ridge that fills the mile between the Stickles would appear to be a place to traverse quickly but don't be deceived. In the rain of 1970 it was a soggy, repellent wilderness but on the right sort of day it can be the best part of the fell. Tarn Hill it is called, from the Duddon side, and there can be no more appropriate name in the whole of Lakeland. Within an area of perhaps half a square mile there are at least half a dozen tarns, probably many more. They are pools of no great size and the tiniest ones must disappear during extended periods of sunny weather. Each has a charm that only folk who wander amongst them can appreciate, but you have to feel the sun on your back and have time on your side to be able to enjoy them for what they are.

As you stroll from one tarn to another with the sun reflected on ripples raised by a playful breeze there is a feeling that they might be scattered jewels of a burst necklace that once adorned the gnarled old neck of Stickle Pike. I can think of few better ways of using a sun-drenched summer afternoon than by wandering amongst these little tarns, going nowhere in particular but enjoying each as it comes in unhurried progression. One August we visited five as we ambled south along the ridge, and this in the middle of the record drought of 1976 when the district's water scenery was very much a dwindling asset. An interesting project would be to do an amateur survey and count them. It could be a personal satisfaction to know just how many pools there are, nestling in the folds of Tarn Hill.

That afternoon in 1976 ranks among the most memorable of a truly memorable summer. The display of bogbean and other water flora complemented the sparkle of the wavelets, highlighted by the aerial acrobatics of a greater profusion of dragonflies and damsel-flies than I can ever remember seeing in one spot. Other insects took their turn on the stage. Indeed 1976 has been called the "Year of the Ladybird" with good reason, but on Tarn Hill even the ladybirds were outnumbered by flights of red admirals, helping to splash the ridge with colour. There must have been more of these popular favourites of the butterfly family about the Cumbrian fell country than for many a long year.

When mist drifts across Tarn Hill it would be extremely easy to go astray. The highest point may be not much more than a thousand feet above the nearby sea but when visibility is curtailed you could lose your way here as easily as anywhere in the district. It would be a humiliating experience to come down in the wrong valley from so small and apparently innocuous a hill.

On the west is the dale of the delectable Duddon. On the other side is the little valley of Dunnerdale Beck where a narrow fell road wends its way across the watershed. From the summit of the low pass is the easy route to Stickle Pike, 400 feet above and half a mile distant. Stainton Ground's old quarries remind you that this was once a place of industry.

The name of Stainton Ground is also a reminder that you are in southern Lakeland. Place-names ending in "Ground" are prolific in the Furness region and a brief count shows at least eight in this immediate neighbourhood, a link with sixteenth-century enclosures of lands that were once the property of Furness Abbey. Those original settlers must have had a hard time clearing their "grounds" but they helped to form the landscape that we know today. Their farmsteads remain as monuments to much effort and if their successors were to desert their homes and lands nature would not be long in reclaiming her own.

Bracken flourishes where allowed its freedom. There

are some patches on the eastern slopes below Tarn Hill where you can disappear in a veritable August jungle. One direct descent had its moments of excitement as we tangled with a wild growth that camouflaged the steep, boulder-strewn hillside. Embryo streams show how swamp must have been a problem for the hardy ancestors who first sought to drain their newly claimed settlements. Even on a short walk such terrain can be a trial for those who must insist on deviating from the beaten track and it is certainly no pleasure for those who are obliged to follow their flocks on such uplands. But for walkers who enjoy a little mild exploration there is a vicious kind of enjoyment to be found in seeking a way through such obstacles.

Most folk who take the trouble to set foot on this wedge of land near the entrance to the Duddon valley are probably attracted by the prospect of a fine little summit, easily gained. They will not be disappointed. That Stickle Pike is a popular target, particularly for Sunday afternoon strollers, is not in doubt. On our last visit a patch of vegetation by the summit cairn appeared to be sprouting a profusion of orange-coloured blossom. Alas! Any thoughts of gaining a degree of immortality by having a hitherto undiscovered species of wild flower named after me were soon dashed. The dainty decorations turned out to be nothing more than a scattering of peel from the well-known citrus fruit.

The track from the nearby road is so clearly marked that it is practically impossible to go astray. I wonder what percentage of those who scramble this way bothers to go further? Still, their quarter-mile walk has its merits. Not the least of these is Stickle Tarn. For those unfamiliar with the area—perhaps motorists drawn by an obvious track to a rugged little peak—Stickle Tarn comes as a pleasant surprise. It is quite unsuspected by folk without maps and may well be a greater delight for that reason. Though somewhat overgrown it looks good in its attractive grassy hollow.

The tarn is shaded by the short, sharp rise to the Pike. When the sun reaches down towards the sea, shadows play a game of hide and seek on the reedy waters. That is a good time to make the brief climb, to see the contrasts of light and shade on nearby hills and watch the warm display of sunset in the western sky.

Stickle Pike, for all its lack of stature, has a top to compare with the best. Those who do choose the lazy tourist route gain a real taste of Lakeland's mountain splendour with an absolute minimum of effort, a sampler as it were, and when they stand on this distinctive little top they may, for a moment, know an inkling of the fell walker's driving force. The cairn stands exactly where it should stand: a final plinth of rock rising from the grassy crest is the resting place of a pyramid of stones so that the cairn becomes an extension of the fell. Not for a single moment can you doubt that this is the top.

The view is better, much better, than the small ascent deserves. It should be the reward for a really comprehensive exploration of the surroundings. The land across the Duddon is well seen, but this is as much a vantage point for the coastal lowlands and the sea as for the hills. Nearer to hand scale is the key to an appreciation of the scene. Everything is in miniature but each item is so well proportioned that in a moment you can forget that this is a mini-landscape. Yet it needs only a sheep to wander into view on an adjacent knoll and the illusion is shattered, for then you have a yardstick against which to assess the scale.

The fells of the Duddon are generous in their rewards, grand little hills indeed, and here is one of the best. But when you walk on Stickle Pike you are only playing at fell walking.

11

EXCITING MINIATURES
(Eagle Crag; Mellbreak; Barf; Helm Crag)

The largest mountains in the district do not have the monopoly in crags. Some of the most popular rock-climbing playgrounds are virtually at valley level—which is one reason for their popularity! Climbers with an hour or two to spare can make profitable use of them as practice grounds when they would not have time to head for the high hills. Shepherds Crag is backed by Brown Dodd, the north ridge of Grange Fell. It is the most famous of a whole series of Borrowdale cliffs where the hinterland is rarely above the 2,000-foot mark. Raven Crag at the foot of Thirlmere is a place of genuine verticality where only the most expert of climbers venture, though the 1,500-foot summit is available to walkers who take a roundabout route through plantations. Some of the favourite crags of Langdale are only a short stroll from either of the Dungeon Ghyll hotels, and many more examples are mentioned elsewhere in these pages.

Some little fells have about them an aura of invincibility, enough to make a mere walker seek out their summits and be glad to get there by any route. They are hills that attract the pilgrims of the high summits, walkers who rarely turn to the foothills but always know a good thing when they see it. The following group is a quartet to rank with the best. These are hills which any red-blooded walker will enjoy, though they are of no great height and may even be regarded as a romp for a little evening exercise. In some cases they present a front that looks positively impregnable, but where a route can be found between almost vertical defences the most timid of mountaineers may enjoy a moment of glory.

These are the moments of which memories are made.

EAGLE CRAG

Those who know the place hardly need to be told that Stonethwaite occupies an outstandingly beautiful fold in the hills, a place whose beauty is outstanding even in the rare surroundings of England's Lake District. The little hamlet sits beside a sparkling beck, lively with water fresh from the hills—too lively when the skies open above the heart of the fell country. Then the valley fills with an impatient liquid roar as streams and gills are no longer able to contain the flow. In 1966 Stonethwaite Beck burst its banks and places in the valley were flooded to a depth of ten feet. Borrowdale became a disaster area.

On either side are steep fellsides clothed with the varied green of many a tree, broken by crag and scree and decorated by cascades more often heard than seen. Yet the floor of the vale is flat enough and although rock and stones lie not far beneath the surface there is a pastoral quality about the scenery. I first saw Stonethwaite, briefly, when bound for the Scafells by way of Rosthwaite Fell and Glaramara. With a long day ahead there was hardly time to loiter in the valley, but the walk-in from Rosthwaite provided an opportunity to stare at one noble object that peered through the portals of Stonethwaite in the direction of Borrowdale: Eagle Crag.

The bold, abrupt pyramid often arrests the gaze of travellers in the main valley and they enjoy a fleeting peep before resuming their briefly interrupted progress. Walkers may make a mental note and indulge in a well-intentioned resolve to climb it some day but so often Eagle Crag takes on the role of a Cinderella, frequently admired but soon forgotten amid the pressing demands of higher fells which can be linked with other worthwhile objectives to make a full and satisfying day on the tops.

Eagle Crag can be used as a stepping stone to High Raise, pre-eminent in the central mass of fell country north of Langdale, but after such an exciting start all else is anticlimax. You *can* make a long day of it from Stonethwaite, linking together much of the sprawling hinterland, but the quality of the walking can be disappointing when the main drama lies in the first mile or so. Eagle

Crag, with its partner Sergeant Crag, are classic examples of small fells best explored on a sunny afternoon and reserved for the off-day between the longer walks that so often take precedence. Those full fell-days may make good talking points in the long winter evenings but little Eagle Crag can leave a more lasting impression on the memory.

The fell presents a fierce front to Stonethwaite. Perhaps that is why so many walkers pass it by. Unless you are armed with prior knowledge the immediate reaction must be that only rock climbers are likely to gain any reward on those crags. A walk to the summit by the back door would be an unappealing prospect even when the final view is likely to be good—and it is—but there is a way by which walkers may safely negotiate all the obstacles. Rock climbers do find excitement there, but the humble walker may have a share of the spoils. The way is steep, it is short, but it is also exceedingly sweet.

Eagle Crag is the final buttress of High Raise in this direction. It is bounded by Greenup Gill on the east and the long trough of Langstrath to the west. The two valleys are drained by becks that meet in a confluence of real charm under the very toes of the aggressive little fell. These watercourses are chains of pools, places of popular resort in the best of the summer months. A camp site that hugs the banks of Stonethwaite Beck almost to the watersmeet must rank as one of the best-situated venues for campers in the whole district.

Where the two streams meet is an island whose name is a direct link with the Middle Ages. Smithymire Island is the site of a medieval bloomery where monks based at Furness Abbey extracted iron from ore, possibly won from deposits mined at Ore Gap between Bowfell and Esk Pike, right at the head of Langstrath. Some authorities suggest that ore was carried over Ore Gap or Esk Hause from mines in Eskdale—by pack horses of course—for the monks were well practised as tradesmen.

Late in the twelfth century Langstrath became the property of Fountains Abbey in Yorkshire and the monks of that foundation used the adjacent fells for grazing their sheep and cattle. Furness Abbey retained Borrowdale. In later years there was some dispute over the ownership of Stonethwaite which became a sort of No-man's-land, encroached upon by both landlords. The settlement in the short connecting valley was attached to Fountains in the original agreement of 1211. One can imagine heated arguments between the monks who colonized these outposts, and the Abbot of Furness certainly had strong feelings on the matter. He considered Stonethwaite to be a part of Borrowdale, rather than Langstrath, and regarded the dairy farm there as a lucrative source of income—income which should be coming his way!

When those monks of bygone days turned to look at Eagle Crag it was probably with thoughts of the dangers that the precipice represented as far as their stock was concerned. Even so, the scene must have been impressed on their minds as one of God's more remarkable pieces of handiwork. The buttresses in some way echo the verticalities of the Langdale Pikes, which enjoy a similar sort of relationship with High Raise at the other side of the plateau. From the valley both have a startling individuality, but when you stand on top it becomes obvious that they are one-sided mountains. An abrupt plunge to the valley is counterbalanced by a gradual rise to a main summit which lies far back.

Eagle Crag and Sergeant Crag are hardly serious rivals to the Langdale group but in just one respect they do enjoy a certain superiority over their more famous cousins. With the distinct valleys of Langstrath and Greenup Gill cutting back on either side they do manage to stand proud of the main mass to some extent. If only for this reason it would be a pity if there was no way in which a direct ascent from Stonethwaite was possible. There is a route, and it presents an excellent opportunity for a little exploration on that sunny afternoon in summer.

On just such a day we chose to take a closer look at the fell in the late seventies. The sun shone pleasantly as we ventured upon the bracken slopes below the crag but it soon became obvious that this was not entirely a blessing. A cooling breeze would have been an asset on so steep a fellside. To make matters worse, the midge population of Stonethwaite was extremely active.

There was a warning of the trials in store even before we left the valley track. We had paused at the confluence of Langstrath Beck and Greenup Gill. A deep green pool in a channel of rock shadowed by trees makes the scene here. Tiny swards of sheep-mown grass, like miniature lawns set in a wild rock-garden, overlook the little gorge. We stood and gazed, listening to the cooling gush of water in the shady depths. Just the place for a picnic, it seemed, but not for long. Spiralling clouds of voracious insects made dallying an indulgence fraught with hazard. We turned to face Eagle Crag and hurried away in search of respite. It was a forlorn hope. These tiny relatives of the mosquito were out in force, waiting to pounce whenever we paused for breath. There is nothing quite like a brigade of blood-thirsty midges for prompting a speedy progress up a mountainside. We shot uphill with an alacrity that had nothing to do with the usual joys of fell walking, leaving a trail of perspiration in our wake. At the top a strong cool breeze was met with cries of heartfelt gladness.

In spite of all this unintended haste the climb did have its moments of interest, though they did not come clearly into focus until we sat at the summit to enjoy them in retrospect. Without the August plague the route would be a joy to follow where it traces a way through outcrops and minor crags, using grassy shelves above the steepest rock to advantage. There are some spectacular views of Lang-strath and of Stonethwaite's valley from some of the rocky parapets.

The main face of Eagle Crag is passed on its right (look-ing towards the mountain). The precipice is startlingly sheer, even appearing to overhang. Away to our left, out of sight but within hearing, a couple of cragsmen were at work, proof that we did not have the fell to ourselves. Though the valleys were busy with purposeful walkers, this was the only evidence of any other human being anywhere on the fell. Sheep there were, of course, though we saw none on the rocky terraces. Down amongst the bracken their heads had a comical appearance as they peered down over the rocks or thick bracken like crotchety old grandads disturbed in their afternoon siesta.

The summit is rock, a wide slab set at an angle amidst grass and bilberry, with a little cairn on the highest edge. There is no indication of the precipice that is Eagle Crag's glory. The contrast in views, east and west, is marked. Ullscarf, Greenup Edge and High Raise are dull, lacking in inspiration, but the head of Greenup Gill—if you walk far enough east to see it—is an interesting place of undulating moraines. To the west is a marvellous panorama of peaks, a display to make the mouth water, with a foreground of bumps and dips that is Rosthwaite Fell.

By one definition Eagle Crag is not a mountain, but 2,000 feet is an arbitrary criterion. This little fell is not much more than 1,600 feet high. It may lack stature yet it fairly bristles with rock and character. For me it is every bit a mountain in miniature, much more so than many a rounded hump a thousand feet higher. Good stuff goes in small space they say, and here is a perfect example of that dictum.

MELLBREAK

Mellbreak is a scene stealer. Drive into the Vale of Lorton and, whether you turn towards Loweswater or the fair valley of Buttermere, this little mountain catches your eye and holds your attention as few fells do. It is not very high, but it looks like a mountain and that is good enough for me. There is a great deal of magnificent mountain scenery around Buttermere, one of the finest dales in almost every respect, but as an individual fell rather than part of a composite picture Mellbreak can hardly be bettered. It stands like a cornerstone between the valleys of Buttermere and Loweswater, far enough from the high fells to avoid comparison in terms of height. Admittedly it faces Grasmoor, more than a thousand feet higher across Crummock Water, and Whiteside too is a comparative giant, but when you approach Lorton these massive hills are out of your line of sight. They may well be the major fells in this part of Buttermere but the nearer you come the less they intrude because by now Mellbreak has your attention and the competition is behind your back, and too near to create a really distinctive individual impression. And in any case, once Mellbreak has your attention it holds it; you can have eyes for little else.

This is the essential Mellbreak. From the Buttermere road, the inevitable viewpoint for any traveller on wheels, the fell is at exactly the right distance to look its best. If you go as far as Lanthwaite Green where the road has climbed a couple of hundred feet above the lake the dimension of depth is added to the view and there is no doubt that you are looking at a very fine hill indeed, a memorable outline framing a dark and craggy façade.

It is just along here, where the foreground of trees gives way to open ground, that Mellbreak and Crummock Water occasionally combine to produce one of the most outstanding moments of mountain and lake scenery that anyone could wish to experience, and all without leaving the car. Mellbreak on its own may be a scene stealer—but in the right conditions, at the right time, and with help from the lake, it is a traffic stopper. I know. I've seen it happen.

It was late in July and possibly the finest morning of a superb summer. For day after day there had been hardly a hint of breeze and Crummock Water resembled a sheet of finely polished glass, a silvered mirror to touch the craftsman's heart in any glazier but on a scale such as only heaven can command. We were driving up to Gatesgarth but the journey came to a premature halt the moment the lake slid into the picture beyond the trees of Lanthwaite Wood. A second Mellbreak burst upon the scene, an inverted image etched with startling clarity on still waters at the toes of the real thing. We did have cameras but the immediate impression was so overwhelming that we never thought to use them—a pity! A photograph could well have been displayed either way up and I am sure that no one would have been any the wiser, as long as the near side of the lake had been kept clear of the viewfinder. Cars lined the road but we never noticed this—until we tried to drive on. In this moment of perfection folk stared like fish gazing from an aquarium, as well they might, and I have no photographic record to convince me that it was true.

Perhaps that is for the best. Maybe memory transcends any factual record—though the traffic jam was real enough.

The view across Crummock Water gives one picture of an exciting mini-mountain, and a very distinctive picture it is too, even on dull, cloudy days when grey water seems to extend the dark sweep of the far fellside. The fell is low enough, and near enough to the sea-board rim of the Cumbrian mountains to escape the clouds on some of the occasions when the central core of high land is lost in mist, and map and compass are an inescapable and essential fact of life for major expeditions on the fells. There is no mistaking Mellbreak. A short ridge raised against the sky looks for all the world like a gigantic and aged backless settee whose springs have gone in the middle. The central depression allows two summits, the southern one being slightly the higher at 1,676 feet, but it is the northern end that dominates Loweswater. It looks particularly good from the lower slopes opposite and it is well worth a traverse of Darling Fell and Low Fell just for the view of this towering rocky nose. But Mellbreak looks good from any road in the area.

I suppose that few will challenge a statement that the northern top with its dramatically over-steepened end receives more visitors than its higher twin. The connecting ridge that looks so inviting from the Buttermere road is something of a sham and proves to be a wide plateau, rather a disappointment when seen at closer quarters, so that there is little encouragement to continue, especially if you have to retrace your steps to Loweswater. Yet it can be a worthwhile addition to your walk if you keep to the Buttermere edge and combine it with a descent to Mosedale where a good track above the marshes returns you to your starting point and introduces an infrequently visited valley. When you see Mellbreak from this side you might be looking at a different mountain. Of course, if you climb Hen Comb or any of the other Loweswater Fells the familiar outline of the ridge-top is easily recognized, but the flank overlooking Mosedale bears no comparison with the fell as seen from the east.

This Mosedale side of Mellbreak is usually left alone. The face overlooking Crummock Water or the abrupt northern end, both excessively steepened as a result of glacial action, give the fell its character though they may not present the whole picture. Here is the rock, the excitement, the inspiring views. To gaze out across the twin lakes is to look inwards towards the heart of the fell district. Buttermere, nestling amid some of Lakeland's finest walking country, captures all your attention from the summit. Crummock Water is hidden but a short stroll brings it into view.

A curiosity of the Crummock Water slope is that here is repeated in modest fashion the pattern seen in the next two valleys to the south. Ennerdale and Wasdale have splendid lakeside walks below a steep flank of fell, and on the same side too. Only the Ullswater flank of Place Fell can be compared with these three but that is a walk of a different and quite unsurpassable character. The level of Crummock Water has been raised slightly to help supply West Cumbria's water needs but the shoreline remains unspoilt, including the little promontory of The Pele. There is a tradition that a pele tower once stood here. This is so much in the past that the stones were used to build a farm which in turn became ruined and forgotten. Only the name remains as a reminder of a forgotten piece of minor history. Further south is another promontory, better known because it looks so good on the map—Low Ling Crag is almost an island. Fortunately the West Cumbrian Water Authority has stopped short of destroying this neat little feature.

By far the best way of climbing Mellbreak is to tackle the northern end. At the outset there is a heap of rough scree but once this has been negotiated the route is a joy to follow. Not so long ago we set out from Kirkstile and enjoyed a really memorable outing. Before leaving the intakes we tangled with a production crew filming sheepdogs at work for a television programme. There was a suggestion of rain in the air but it never came to much and the sun eventually won an uneven battle and provided us with a splendid afternoon.

I remember looking out across the Vale of Lorton from a heathery perch round about the half-way mark and seeing a rainbow below our feet, suspended above green pastures near Kirkstile. There was a peculiar sense of unreality in the scene, with the rainbow fading and returning several times over a period of perhaps half an hour. A few drops of rain splashed our faces, but without conviction, and a decision to leave cagoules in our packs proved well founded.

From below the predominant feature of this climb would appear to be rock but all the ledges and platforms are hidden from view and in the main our memories are of heather. You climb above the steepness and an inviting track, far too short, leads you in a few easy strides to the cairn. The only disappointment is that the top is not the summit of the fell, which would be fitting. It is something of an anticlimax to have to cross those undistinguished acres of plateau to reach a high point the best part of a mile distant, where grassy surroundings lack the immediacy of that first cairn, an island in the heather. Nevertheless, conscientious walkers feel in honour bound to make the crossing, on a first ascent anyway.

It would be satisfying to conclude by telling of a happy interlude centred on the traditional opening of lunch packets, but it was not to be. A mysterious zinging sound reminiscent of that high-pitched buzz sometimes heard from power-lines turned out to be caused by a small but insistent party of harrying hornets hovering over the cairn, not the best of company when you intend to broach a parcel of jam butties. Muttering vaguely about discretion and valour we moved off with unseemly haste. Lunch would be on the south top after all. There are limits to the amount of excitement that even the most ardent fell walkers will accept when they reach their peaks!

BARF

I suppose everyone who knows northern Lakeland is familiar with the whitened stone sentinel that stands on a crumbling pedestal guarding the Swan Hotel at the head of Bassenthwaite Lake. Many a visitor to the area raises a curious glance and perhaps, following a line of enquiry, learns of a connection with the hotel and possibly a version of the legend of how the petrified Bishop came to rest on that forbidding chunk of mountainside. More persistent visitors may also trace the Bishop's footsteps to the 700-foot contour and come away surprised that the old fellow could manage to climb even as far as that before being committed to an eternal stony vigil. Their sympathies are likely to turn to the Bishop's Clerk who was content to watch the proceedings from a position of security at the foot of Beckstones Gill.

Such folk may greet with incredulity any statement that a route can be followed beyond the Bishop's airy platform. Only determined walkers bother to seek the summit of the parent hill, though a well-worn trod is witness to the fact that this hardier breed is a quite considerable minority. The Bishop of Barf may be best known as a popular tourist landmark and a gratuitous advertisement for the Swan Hotel, but the precipitous fellside on which he stands regularly attracts fell walkers who feel that here is one walk that they really must get out of their system, to be done once and then forgotten. In fact no hill is ever as steep as it looks, seen face-on. Foreshortening exaggerates the angle and in this case the rise from the road to the summit is just over 1,200 feet in a horizontal distance of two fifths of a mile (2,112 feet). This makes the average gradient little more than one in two. Mind you, that is just an average and it really is much steeper in places. If it still doesn't sound too bad, try it on a hot afternoon. I've known people draw a parallel with the north face of the Eiger!

You can reach the top without the excitements of this energetic, rocky scramble. A route which starts up Beckstones Gill will get you there in a roundabout way but it includes encounters with Forestry Commission plantations and a stretch of rough grassland, a combination which hardly produces the flavour of true fell walking. Still, the Beckstones Plantation is a cooler proposition than the open fell on a really hot day, and when rain threatens there is much to be said for a walk through the trees. The perpetual pine needles certainly muffle the sound of traffic from the busy road below. We once came down this way from Barf after walking over from the Whinlatter area and one of us was nearly lost when he went ahead and took a wrong turning. Forest ways can be like that.

Barf is really part of Lord's Seat—the end of its east ridge sawn off rather abruptly by a passing glacier in the last ice age. It is a slate hill, surprisingly for such a rugged upstart. Lord's Seat is much more typical of this kind of country and is the highest point of a quartet of small hills north of the Whinlatter Pass, the others being Whinlatter Fell, Broom Fell and Graystones. They form a neat group round the hidden valley of Aiken Beck. With its series of connecting ridges this would be an attractive little horseshoe route if it was not interrupted by the plantations of Thornthwaite Forest. In the early sixties two of us did this round as an afternoon stroll, an unusual and varied walk which included the novelty of a little route-finding among trees and along the forest roads. The gentle pull up to Lord's Seat after the eclipse of the Whinlatter trees was a welcome moment, with the bonus of a rich bounty of bilberries to help us over the forest fence.

We missed out Barf that day. It is out on a limb, an indistinct heathery ridge, a journey from an unruffled and easy-going parent to a wild upstart of an offspring. In mist this is no place for strangers—the sudden drop to Bassenthwaite Lake allows no second chance. The sheer, rocky character of the east face is best appreciated from across the lake. It stands out vividly as the only section of bare fell in four miles of conifer-clad hillside. It is too steep for the profitable cultivation of trees so maybe the crags have been the saviour of Barf.

Forestry is the modern industry hereabouts. In the past minerals have been won from the fell at Thornthwaite. The miners mainly brought out the ores of galena (lead) and blende (zinc) over a period of many years, but the mines finally closed early in the present century. Most of the works were between the road and the old railway. Now even the trains are a thing of the past, but the road is busier than ever and is likely to become more so. Controversial improvements have encouraged heavy transport along the A66, giving it almost the status of a motorway in a National Park.

You must climb a long way up Barf to escape the noise of traffic. Half a dozen years ago we climbed above the last wall of crag before this unwelcome sound was lost. Then we found an excellent couch in luxuriant bilberries where we were able to relax in peaceful comfort and look at the world below our feet.

It was a scorching day. The start brought to mind the familiar comment, "One step up, two steps back!" for the shifting slate scree provides as mobile a footing as only loose scree can. I doubt if it could lie at a steeper angle. Even where the slate is attached to the mountain it is only a nominal attachment and it needs treating with respect. You don't pull at handholds in slate, you push—pressing the stuff into place. Above the scree came a scramble up a tiny gully, a heathery platform, a proud little rowan like a lonely arboreal sculpture shaped with a touch of nature's artistry; these are good memories. Slape Crag seems to bar the way but a rake on the left is the key. Then an airy traverse above the final line of rock leads to the viewpoint *par excellence*.

The summit Barf has good views across the lake but the bed of bilberries has my vote on a sunny afternoon. Here is comfort that the thinly grassed top lacks. Below are the hotel and the nearby houses, toys in a doll's garden. Awareness of space beneath your feet would seem to bring every detail sharply into focus. The lake is an inland sea only waiting the turn of the tide to flood the flatlands at its head. We looked beyond to see at the far end members of the yachting club slowly sally forth in model boats, making placid patterns on the still water, water that can crumple like corrugated cardboard when the Lakeland air decides to move with a will.

This lowland landscape with its frame of trees and rich pastures is the foreground to one of the most satisfyingly composed mountain groups in the country and here, just below the summit of a comparatively minor fell, is as good a place as any for an appraisal of the overall picture. Skiddaw sits majestically, head and shoulders above his courtiers. Carl Side and Dodd kneel before him and standing deferentially on either side are Jenkin Hill and the grassy ridge of Long Side Edge and Ullock Pike. Smooth, grassy slopes with a wainscot of trees on Dodd and the lower reach of Long Side lead in ordered progression to the climax—England's fourth-highest mountain. On Barf, with the top of our own hill just a few short strides away, we sat at exactly the right height to see the Skiddaw fells in perfection, a grandstand view of northern Lakeland at its best.

HELM CRAG

It would seem that everyone who knows the Lake District knows Helm Crag. Young and old, agile and infirm, they all know the rugged little hill that stands behind the village of Grasmere. They may not have climbed it, they may have no intention of ever setting foot on it, but they know where it is though they may have no interest in any other fell in the district. It could be that Helm Crag is the best-known fell of all, for folk who would be hard put to name Scafell Pike as the highest land in England would quickly put a name to Grasmere's mini-mountain—but often enough the name would not be Helm Crag. The name that enjoys the popular acclaim refers to a set-piece of natural rock sculpture that crowns the end of the short summit ridge: the Lion and the Lamb.

Helm Crag is not quite the nearest fell to Grasmere. Silver How's summit is nearer by about a quarter of a mile, but Helm Crag is more closely associated with the village than any other hill. Despite its modest altitude it contrives to dominate the place with almost a cheeky arrogance. At the other side of the A591 trunk road over Dunmail Raise is Seat Sandal, almost twice as high, but folk look at little Helm Crag and call it a mountain and ignore the rather dull grassy mound across the way. Height is not everything in mountain scenery, quite obviously. Appearance has so much to say and Helm Crag has something that many a mountain giant would be glad to own, a commanding presence and a rugged, crenellated crest, and it is all in the shop window, always on view from a popular tourist centre and from one of the busiest roads in the district. You cannot cross Dunmail Raise without being aware of Helm Crag.

Helm Crag is such a popular hill and so small in compass that it is difficult to envisage a route away from the inevitable company, especially during the summer months. Not the sort of place for a lone walker to indulge his craving for solitude, you would think, but it has always seemed to me that there is scope for a little solitary exploration even here. For a long time I promised myself that I would climb the east face of this little fell. The unusual lay-out of the top is such that I felt sure that this approach would reveal its peculiar features in the most satisfactory way possible, even though I knew what to expect. For one reason or another the plan had been put by, but constant postponements did nothing to diminish the desire and eventually—inevitably, I suppose—the plan was turned into action.

One Saturday afternoon I took Sarah up Stone Arthur. It was a short walk that we both enjoyed, but with a cold wind to test our enthusiasm we had no inclination to linger at the top and quite soon we were back in Grasmere. With half the afternoon still before me the obvious "fill-in" sprang quickly to mind and before anyone could suggest an alternative for the vacant hours I left Sarah with mother and departed, saying, "I'll see you in a couple of hours. I'm going up Helm Crag."

I reached the open fell below Raven Crag where the swooping and swerving of swallows symbolized the freedom to be found away from the restrictions of the walled pastures. Looking up, I took a deep breath and set off. As compensation for the exertion I reckoned that here was one place where the phrase "having the hill to yourself" would be of real meaning. Surely no one else would be at large on this steep, untracked fellside? But no! Half-way up I met another walker coming down. I have rarely seen anyone look quite as astonished. He was taking a short cut to his car, he told me. I replied that I was taking a short cut to the top, which seemed to be an appropriate enough response at the time. "Rather you than me!" he commented in a tone of voice that seemed to infer that he was in the company of a lunatic—or at the very least, an idiot—but was too polite to say as much. We went our separate ways.

But the ascent was easier than might be expected. The climb is steep, of course, but there is not much of it and when you break new ground, away from the fixed lines of tracks and footpaths, there is always an abundance of interest to make the way seem short. This is one of the great joys of the fell country. Whereas in the lowlands you are perforce restricted to well-trodden ways because of the concentrated usage of land, on the open fell you can escape the restraint of fences, walls and hedges. You have the freedom to get away from the tracks and find your own way, to enjoy the thrill of small-scale adventure and often you have the feeling that you are walking where no man has walked before. More than likely you are mistaken, of course. In the most unlikely spots I have come across discarded boot-heels and worse—there is a heap of scrap metal high on the western scree-slopes of Skiddaw, and I can only suppose that this is the result of cleaning-up operations on that much-abused summit. But apart from such bizarre evidence of human passage there can be hardly a single square yard of walkable, unenclosed Lakeland that has not been trodden by a shepherd at some time or other. However, we can all enjoy our fantasies. I know that some of my most enjoyable mountain days have come when I have truly left the beaten track, and it is so easy to do.

On Helm Crag, with gentle sunshine to brighten the way ahead and a brisk breeze to cool the engine, I was in my element. I paused to watch a circling monoplane make several passes over the bowl of Grasmere, coming close enough for me to read the registration figures before it turned with a noisy roar to cross Dunmail Raise and vanish in the direction of Thirlmere. In the ensuing silence came a lonely mewing and I turned to see a buzzard swing gently into view from behind Raven Crag and soar from below to hang high above my head before drifting away beyond the rocky silhouette of the fell. I leaned against a rock and watched it reappear and give a couple of repeat performances as though to say, "Look how easy it is. How much more satisfying than the clumsy, mechanical efforts of that silly aeroplane." And I could only nod my head in agreement.

Threading my way through broken crags I found with astonishment that I was there, almost before getting into my stride. There is no mistaking the top of Helm Crag. The summit ridge—where the track over the top lies—has a duplicate a short distance to the east, across a hollow that is a wilderness of boulders. Beyond is a third ridge, the best of the lot really because you can walk along its narrow crest with the immediate plunge of the east face below your elbow. This was where I had arrived and I paused on the rim to gaze into a deep trough, for all the world like the dry ditch of some medieval castle.

There is a wild quality about the top of Helm Crag that makes this one of the most satisfying summits of all, especially when the place is as deserted as it was then, late on a Saturday afternoon. After the customary half-hour of desultory exploration I headed for the highest rocks and scrambled to the crest of the pinnacle, a perch that certainly humours any inclination to be "king of the castle". These north-west rocks have a variety of names. To some they are the Lion and the Lamb for though the official Lion and Lamb is the group at the other end of the ridge this formation shows a more realistic resemblance from along the Dunmail road. They are also known as the Howitzer or the Old Lady at the Organ —with a certain lack of respect we used to call them Ted Heath at the Piano. You have to keep your eyes open on the descent from Dunmail Raise to recognize these set pieces, but whatever you see it is always the same group. Only the viewpoint changes.

My afternoon ended with a trot down to Grasmere, the first time on this so-called tourist track for some years. How it has been hacked to pieces! Near Jackdaw Crag the ravages of human erosion are appalling. For a few years we have avoided the more popular ways as much as possible but a couple of minutes here brought home to me the extent of their deterioration by over-use as nothing else could. And there are so very many places where tracks remain unspoilt and undamaged as they have done for years, as well as places where there are no tracks at all and still provide good walking. They will always be there for the discerning minority. The multitude will always head for the aptly named honeypots because, let's face it, they are good places to see.

The track by Jackdaw Crag was the only sour moment in an otherwise marvellous afternoon. A much happier final note came as I strolled into Grasmere down the Easedale lane, a by-way alive with birdlife where a veritable profusion of blue tits made me forget, at least for the time being, those scars above the intakes.

12

WEST OF ULLSWATER
(Foothills of the Helvellyn Range)

Between Nab Scar and Clough Head are some thirteen
miles of high-level ridge walking, most of it over 2,000 feet
and surpassing 3,000 feet twice in the neighbourhood of
Helvellyn. It is one of the longest continuously high-level
ridge routes in the district and if anything could be called
the Backbone of the Lakeland Fells, then this is it. With
only one appreciable drop—where the contours fall just
below 2,000 feet at Grisedale Tarn—this is not a really
arduous walk despite its length and it links three mountain groups: Fairfield, Helvellyn and the Dods. Yet I
hardly think it is stretching a point too much to label the
three groups under one general heading, the Helvellyn
Range. Helvellyn is the highest point. It has been the first
fell for many a fell-walking enthusiast, myself included, it
is the only fell for numerous transient visitors, and if you
walk the range from end to end you can hardly avoid its
summit even if you wanted to—which seems highly unlikely. If you talk of the Helvellyn Range I always think of
the whole highland mass between the A591 road that
crosses Dunmail Raise and the long dale that contains
Ullswater. It is a range that owns some of the finest mountains in the land.

The roof-top axis of this range lies well to the west so
that as you travel north from Dunmail Raise the high
watershed is poised above your right shoulder. There are
no foothills here. Only to the south of the pass is there
anything that falls into such a category. Seat Sandal is
high as Lakeland foothills come but in the face of a ridge
with an average height of some 2,500 feet it undeniably is
a foothill. Further south are the more modest heights of
Stone Arthur and Nab Scar. A stranger might look at this

side of the range and see little to get excited about, just the vast sweep of a rather plain grassy fellside broken by an occasional watercourse and stretching into the distance where its toes are neatly tucked into a counterpane of evergreen plantations, but if he should cross to the east he would be in a different world. From Patterdale and the shores of Ullswater you see deep, far-reaching valleys leading west into a tumble of exciting peaks and ridges. Now the idea of a single unified mountain group never enters the mind. You have to cross the lake and climb the eastern fells to have a view of the long backbone of a skyline where these side valleys have their birth.

Some of the valleys are lonely places where only dedicated walkers and climbers bother to go. Only one of them can truly be called a place of popular resort. That is Grisedale, the gateway to Helvellyn and, almost incidentally, the best foot pass between Patterdale and Grasmere. But you can be sure that most of the walkers who set foot in Grisedale have their sights set on Striding Edge and Helvellyn. There are other ways to reach the roof of eastern Lakeland, some of much more continuous interest than England's most famous arête which is, after all, only a few hundred yards long, but the majority does not want to know. May we be thankful for this lack of vision. We have been in Ruthwaite Cove in the midst of some of the wildest corrie scenery that the Lake District can provide and seen no sign of any human other than ourselves. We have scrambled up to Nethermost Pike and looked across Nethermost Cove to see Striding Edge adorned with tiny figures like a telegraph cable burdened with swallows in autumn. Striding Edge is good. There is no doubt about that—but there are other places in this west-of-Ullswater region that cry out to be visited. You have only to drive along the lakeside road to realize that.

This is where the Helvellyn foothills lie. The high watershed stands well back from the lake but it throws out a series of ridges that reach virtually to the water's edge, truncated spurs that do their utmost to block the way to motor traffic altogether. When the great glacial masses were hard at work carving the district into the exciting

Cow Bridge at Hartsop

Ullswater from Keldas

The summit of Birkett Fell. Thick mist covers Ullswater and the Eden valley; in the distance the Pennines

Black Combe from the shore at Silecroft

Near the summit of Whiteside Pike, Selside. Exposed rock shows interesting strata

Sadgill, Longsleddale

A view of the Helvellyn Dods from the grassy slopes of Souther Fell

Binsey crowned by an ancient cairn, with Skiddaw beyond

Raven Crag above Thirlmere's dam

Castle Crag, early British fort above Thirlmere. To the right of the
walker is the steep cleft of the Shoulthwaite valley

Silver How from Grasmere's island

Haystacks above the pines and flags of Warnscale Bottom

The precipitous head of Swindale, looking towards Selside Pike

Old survey device on Branstree above Haweswater

topographical extravaganza that we know today, these ridges were shorn off at their roots. The ice departed and Ullswater came into being, and the centuries of gentler erosion that followed rounded off some of the harsher excesses of the glaciers so that vegetation could get to grips with the landscape and prepare the way for trees. And therein lies the delight of the Ullswater scene, a unique combination of rock, open fell, woodland and water that brings the band of Ullswater worshippers back to their favourite valley year after year. There are those who swear that Ullswater and Patterdale are worth all England else—never mind what Caldbeck folk might say.

All the way from Ullswater to Brotherswater the road is flanked on the west by foothills of the finest character. They hug the roadside so effectively that often they seem much higher than they really are. In fact some of these hills are surprisingly easy in ascent, considered simply in terms of vertical feet to be climbed. The surface of Ullswater is nearly 500 feet above the level of the sea so you have a built-in start that ridicules the impressive altitude of some of these summits. Where else can you reach a 1,000-foot top—such as Keldas—with only 500 feet of effort? But don't be fooled by such beguiling figures. There are crags around here too and some of the little fells hold hazardous traps waiting to catch the unwary. Mist brings problems in route-finding to challenge the best of us when we walk without foresight and care.

The foothills start just above Brotherswater and the first I ever set foot on was Hartsop-above-How—Gill Crag if you wish to air local knowledge, or familiarity with an authoritative guidebook. You can usually rely upon Wainwright for accuracy. The official name is an odd sort of mouthful, something of an enigma until you think about it. The How is the hill and the village of Hartsop is below it. Obviously the reverse must hold true: the How is above Hartsop, but it is a clumsy sort of appellation none the less.

Three of us came down from Hart Crag having done the round of Deepdale over St Sunday Crag and Fairfield. It rained. What a wealth of meaning there is in those two words! We had enjoyed one of the best sort of days, plenty

of sunshine but tempered by a cooling breeze, and I remember a leisurely progress on St Sunday Crag where a
fine crop of bilberries discouraged any ideas of a speedy
ascent. I have never been one for undue haste on the fells
anyway and this day was no exception. We ambled round
the ridge and it was late afternoon when we crossed
Hartsop-above-How, just as the weather broke. A little
more speed earlier on and we would have missed the
soaking that followed. With the end of the walk so near we
hardly thought it necessary to dig out the wet-weather
gear—until it was too late. Some twenty minutes after the
first heavy raindrops fell we were back in the car, as wet as
it is possible to be short of jumping into a bath fully
clothed. My diary notes "a spot of good old Lakeland rain",
a phrase endowed with latent significance for those who
know.

Hartsop-above-How is bounded by two of Lakeland's
finest dales, places for the connoisseur. Deepdale and
Dovedale are becoming better known but you can still
wander there and be free from the intrusion of unseemly
crowds. You have only to take a few strides away from the
main valley and you are in a world apart. Sometimes
holiday-makers who have not been converted to the fell
walker's way of life do venture a short way into these
hidden worlds but they never move far from their cars and
sometimes have little interest in the detail of their
surroundings.

There comes to mind an interlude by Goldrill Beck near
Brotherswater. Standing there with the slopes of Hartsop-
above-How at my back I watched a dipper patrolling the
stream. It was fascinating to watch the simple, unselfcon-
scious performance as the bird returned from each sortie to
alight on the same water-washed pedestal, bob a couple of
times, hop across the ripples to another stone, then fly up
to its nest only a few yards from where I stood. Nearby
picnickers chattered and joked, oblivious of anything
worthy of their attention. Perhaps that is as it should be.
Not everyone would be content to let the local wildlife go
about its business unmolested, but nevertheless in even
the busiest of places there is an untold wealth of interest

for those who have the inclination to look and the patience
to wait.

On the north side of Deepdale the ridge of St Sunday
Crag ends with a gem of a minor fell, Arnison Crag. This is
one of those little hills that are nothing out of the ordinary
until you look at the summit. Here is a fine target for an
evening walk; rocky, elevated from its ridge, and it follows
the recurrent pattern of so many foothills west of the upper
reach of Ullswater in the excellence of its view of the lake.
You don't even have to climb up there to appreciate that it
has a spark of individuality. If you can find time to glance
this way on the drive down from Kirkstone you can hardly
mistake Arnison Crag. We always look for the distinctive
notched crest as we approach Hartsop. It is one of the most
easily recognized summits in Lakeland and would not be
out of place on a much larger fell.

We once set off into Deepdale with no real plans in mind
about where we were going. Just up the dale and back, or
had we the time for something more ambitious? It was late
in the afternoon, and with a youngster to consider there
was hardly time to look at a major fell. In the event we
turned up Coldcove Gill and crossed above Aiken Crag to
follow the ups and downs of the short ridge to Arnison
Crag. Other walkers were standing near the summit outcrop and gazing at Ullswater, leaving us free to find a
perch on the highest point—or so we thought. But there
was good reason for avoiding the place like the plague. A
swarm of flying ants was in full possession, picketing the
sun-warmed rocks with the enthusiasm of strikers at a
factory gate. We chose a substitute summit in the form of a
superior-looking cairn on an eminence much lower down
in the direction of Patterdale and later we tangled with
high bracken and boulders we descended to the village.

Arnison Crag is a cub of St Sunday Crag but there is
sufficient separation to make it a worthwhile mini-
mountain. The parent fell has another outlier in this direction, Birks, but this one is hardly distinctive enough to call
for separate identity. If you climb Birks you will probably
go on to visit the major top, but Arnison Crag has enough
going for it to encourage walkers looking for a little even-

ing exercise with the reward of a rocky top and an excellent view, and it is only 800 feet or so above the valley.

The east ridge of Helvellyn holds the classic approach to a famous mountain. We all know Striding Edge, an exciting climax which draws the crowds like the football pools draw the punters. East of the renowned "gap in the wall" the ridge is less known. Birkhouse Moor is the name but though it rises to over 2,300 feet there is little to separate it from its infinitely more illustrious parent and nothing at all to attract walkers for the greater part of its length. Of course it is hardly playing the game to make such a comparison. In truth, it would need an outstanding fell to make any kind of showing in the shadow of Helvellyn.

Yet there is one redeeming feature. Where the ridge has almost reached the lake, just as it seems to have resigned itself to a peaceful demise, it springs to life in the shape of a delightful little summit called Keldas. I have always had a soft spot for Keldas. The name alone seems to have a touch of magic about it, a combination of letters with a soft and musical ring that makes you expect something rather special—Glaramara and Blencathra are just two more from a list of mountain names that are alive with the same quality. If the reality happened to be a dull, run-of-the-mill sort of mound a visit would only result in disappointment but whoever named Keldas was blessed with an unconscious gift for poetry. Surely no one could dream up Keldas out of anything far short of perfection?

Keldas is everything that its name suggests. Its summit is the vantage point *par excellence* for the upper reach of Ullswater and there can be few lakes with viewpoints to equal this in the width and breadth of Lakeland. A foreground of Scots pines provides the frame through which Ullswater shimmers with unbelievable beauty not much more than 500 feet below. When the time comes that Keldas is beyond my reach then the time to call it a day will most certainly have arrived.

You might say that Keldas is the molehill with the most, if you can bring yourself to describe so delectable a little fell in such prosaic terms. Trees, crags, water and view, even a tarn to call its own; they all help to make this tiny corner of Lakeland unforgettable. The tarn lies in the depression which effectively draws the line between the uninspired grass of Birkhouse Moor and Keldas itself. Lanty's Tarn is maybe 150 yards long and less than its length from the summit cairn. A tiny ruined building nearby was a store hut for ice gathered from the tarn in winter in the days before refrigeration. The ice was placed in a deep bowl and an insulation of a few feet of sawdust was sufficient to maintain the supply until the summer months.

Patterdale is St Patrick's Dale. The patron saint of Ireland is supposed to have passed through the valley and paused near Ullswater to perform a series of baptisms. There may be an element of truth in the legend and certainly Keldas has a well named in memory of the saint. St Patrick's Well, beside the road below Hall Bank, is fed by the spring which is reputed to be the water supply used in these ceremonies of so long ago. It is a pleasant story and if true it is nice to think that it all happened in the shadow of dear old Keldas.

North of Keldas is Glenridding and the entrance to the dale of the lead mines. Curiously, the far side of this dale has another minor fell, slightly higher but with much in common with Keldas. This is Glenridding Dod. Again there is a skirt of trees and again there are charming views of the lake. Wherever you go on the slopes above the upper reach of Ullswater the lake views are good. Even the rather uninspiring ridge of Watermillock Common, the next height north, has a splendid long-range vista from its terrace path above Glencoyne Park. If you follow these ridges west—from Glenridding Dod or Watermillock Common—you eventually reach Stybarrow Dod, and in the case of Watermillock Common you pass over Hart Side on the way. A grassy bump north-east of Hart Side was formerly granted a negative sort of distinction, being labelled Nameless Fell by the Ordnance Survey. Now it is Birkett Fell, named in honour of Lord Birkett in memory of his efforts in the service of Ullswater. One cannot help but think it a pity that so unprepossessing a hill should be chosen to commemorate the great man.

North and east there is a gradual decline with only Gowbarrow Fell and the twins of Great and Little Mell Fells to remind you that this is the verge of the fell country. Gowbarrow Fell is famous for its Aira Force but the summit is quite pleasant and its wide heathery ridge leads due south to Green Hill and the obligatory view of the lake. A few years ago I enjoyed a satisfying stroll from Little Mell Fell over Gowbarrow Fell to Aira Force. Not an outstanding walk by any means, in the context of the Ullswater Fells, just a stroll to take advantage of a couple of hours I had to spare in the neighbourhood but it was enjoyable enough in the late summer sunshine and it had the merit of being mostly away from the crowds.

This was a walk which had as motive the express purpose of getting Little Mell Fell out of my system. It is the one and only time I have been up there and in truth I can remember very little about it apart from the grass and a few patches of heather. Perhaps I should have gone across to Great Mell Fell whilst in the vicinity but I didn't, and it is still waiting. Instead, I crossed to Great Meldrum and followed a track along the top of the Ullswater flank, revelling in view of the lake and basking in the sun with my shirt tied around my waist. Not until Gowbarrow Fell did I meet anyone and then the crowds increased as I sauntered along the short ridge to Green Hill and headed for Aira Force in the land of coach parties and ice creams.

We recently drove along the Ullswater road and over Kirkstone Pass on an August evening and the place was deserted. The summer had been wet, August especially so, and it seemed that everyone had forsaken the district. Hardly a car was to be seen and the only people were a couple of fishermen taking advantage of an odd hour of sport beside the lake. We stopped for a while and watched a squall race down the Helvellyn Range and sweep across Ullswater following a pattern that must have been persisting most of the day. Yet between these heavy showers the sun filtered through and lit the valley with a curious, gentle light which seemed to lift the landscape out of its drowned, bedraggled daze and bring the mountains to life. Soft banks of mist drifted across distant slopes and obscured the well-known outlines so that we saw the scene anew, like a strange mountain region visited for the first time.

Ullswater is three lakes in one. Three distinct sections, each with its own distinctive qualities, make Ullswater unmistakable and unique. But always there is the back-cloth of fells, different in character on either side of England's second-largest lake. The eastern fells are made relatively aloof by this vast moat but the foothills of the Helvellyn Range are immediately available, splendid targets for the short walk. They seem almost a special provision for the evening stroll. In this respect in more than any other they are outstanding.

13

FOOTHILLS OF THE FRINGE
(Black Combe; Whiteside Pike; Souther Fell; Binsey)

When you approach a mountainous region you expect to see the smallest hills first. In a perfect arrangement they would gradually increase in size as you penetrate beyond the fringe and in the centre you would find a core of high mountains. Such faultless symmetry would not be as aesthetically satisfying as the kind of layout that nature generally contrives. There is pleasure in the unexpected, yet the most apparently haphazard of nature's designs has a pattern, which is why we take pleasure in the natural scene. We look at a view and see—perhaps—a tall tree on one side balanced by a distant mountain group and maybe a stream giving emphasis to one of the other, with a host of minor details to bring life to the whole picture and if the proportions are right we think, "That is good to look at." A photograph with the highest mountain placed centrally is only rarely an artistic success. Flower arrangers observe the same rules within the confines of a vase or a bowl.

If you cross the Yorkshire Pennines east to west you encounter a gradual rise of land until you reach England's main watershed which is set appreciably west of a geometrically placed central line. Beyond is a comparatively sharp decline to the lowlands of Lancashire, not an obvious way of doing things but it is better so. In Cumbria the mountains are balanced about three high points where the land rises above 3,000 feet but there are several geographically separate groups of fells each with its own foothills and even these are not all neatly placed around an individual rim. But, with odd exceptions, the region as a whole is fringed with foothills so that from almost all points of entry it is the small fells that you reach first.

Curiously, two obvious exceptions are diametrically op-
posed, Black Combe in the south-west and Blencathra to
the north-east, but Black Combe is a special case and
Blencathra has its own personal foothill as a buffer
against the outside world. Skiddaw is quite near the rim
too, though not to the same extent as Blencathra.

The fells which form the basis of this chapter are
selected from the four corners of the district. There are
plenty of other small fells of the fringe but these make as
varied a selection as any. Perhaps they may be called
cornerstones of the Lakeland fells, if anything as slight as
a foothill deserves so imposing a title, and certainly they
are fells worth climbing. But that is not a special recommendation. Any fell is worth climbing—at least once,
anyway.

BLACK COMBE

When is a foothill not a foothill? This question is prompted
by the thought that Black Combe is the highest hill for
miles around and it seems inappropriate to describe it as a
foothill. On the other hand Seat Sandal, nearly 500 feet
higher, is included in this book because it is undoubtedly
subservient to Fairfield and Dollywaggon Pike—in fact it
is dwarfed by every summit of the Helvellyn range from
Great Rigg Man to Great Dod. Black Combe, though
lower, can never be considered subservient to anything.
The nearest ground that overtops Black Combe is on
Walna Scar some ten miles away so this is hardly a foothill
in the accepted sense, but it falls short of the 2,000-foot
mark by thirty feet, which makes it a beginner when
compared with Seat Sandal.

Black Combe finds a place here because it is one of a
group of hills which—like the Howgills—are foothills to
the Lakeland fells proper. Nevertheless it is a giant among
foothills and looks every inch a mountain. It rises from the
beginnings of the coastal plain of west Cumbria with the
sea less than a mile from the foot of the south-west slopes
and being a mountain of the coast every inch of its height
counts. If you follow the A595 from Whicham to Bootle you
are very much aware of the brooding presence above your

right shoulder. Great smooth buttresses of heathery hillside sweep down to the edge of the road and if the upper
reaches are swathed in cloud there is a shadowed darkness
about the hill that makes the name Black seem very appropriate indeed, though the fell is most likely named
from the great hollow cut out of the opposite flank—a
black combe indeed seen in shadow against the setting sun
or when topped by a bank of thundery clouds. Deep-cut
watercourses divide the seaward slopes into individual
sections and there is some slight resemblance to the lower
part of Blencathra when observed from the A66 in similar
climatic conditions.

Such a comparison is apt. Both fells are composed of the
same basic material, Skiddaw Slate. This rock lies at the
base of Lakeland's geological structure and surfaces only
in the far north and south. Everything else rests on top of
the ancient slates, including the typically Lakeland formations of the Borrowdale Volcanics which are relative
newcomers in the geological sequence. Quite obviously
Black Combe must join the mountains of the Skiddaw
group as a member of the Founders' Club. These may be
the oldest mountains in the district and it has been
claimed that they are among the oldest hills in the
country.

It is Black Combe's fortune—or misfortune, depending
upon how you look at it—to stand on the fringe. Being so
far from reasonable competition it looks a much greater
fell than it really is, but then the main stamping ground of
those who like to walk the fells is so far away that they
have to go out of their way to climb it. When we drove west
across the southern edge of the district we always turned
right beyond Broughton-in-Furness and followed the Duddon road to Ulpha and points north. Sometimes we did
drive round the coast, or over the fell road towards
Ravenglass, but poor old Black Combe got the cold shoulder until quite recently when I decided that it really was
about time I climbed it.

We had looked at the fell often enough. Visiting Millom
and Silecroft we could hardly miss this great hunk of
upland that dominates the south-western corner of

Cumbria. With the sea so near and the sands of Silecroft ranging along the coast under its western slopes it well deserves to be called the Seaside Mountain. It looms above the Furness coast so that holiday-makers at Grange-over-Sands and even as far afield as Morecambe can turn and see it and maybe they think they are looking at one of Lakeland's highest mountains. Sometimes the more athletic of them decide to take a day away from the seaside and test themselves by climbing to its summit. It is no real test though, because the most popular route to the top is as easy a climb as you can find anywhere. A well-engineered track takes you up from Whicham and you can continue down the other side in the direction of Bootle, and most of the way the gradient is so gentle that there can be hardly any sensation of climbing a mountain at all.

To be honest, I have not walked this route in its entirety but I have followed it in part and this experience, combined with a study of the contours of the O.S. map, provides enough evidence to suggest an easy day out for a family group. My sampler was done in mist and there was never a moment when the track became so indistinct that route finding was anything of a problem. Even so, to reach the summit of a hill that seems especially designed as a vantage point for looking across a wide sweep of southern Lakeland with a seascape to match on the other side is adventure enough for casual visitors from the coastal resorts. A hill crowned by an O.S. column and a windshelter of rough stones, with a deep corrie biting the edge of the summit plateau, gives a feel of the real mountains and the ascent, easy as it is, has a flavour of the fells about it.

They say the view from Black Combe is one of the most far-reaching in the land. I would not know because all I saw on my visit was a curtain of mist and the spray of rain bouncing off the stones of the windshelter as I crouched in its illusory protection to eat my sandwiches. And driven by a fierce wind those raindrops were cold and hard enough to be hail. I had hoped for better conditions but the day had been chosen and I would be unable to return for some time so I decided to make the best of it and climb the fell. There *could* have been a miracle. A lightening of the sky did allow hope of a change in the weather—such things do happen. Some of the best days start dull but bring the reward of a long view from a summit as clouds lift in the afternoon but this time it was not to be. The weather only got worse and I saw little of my mountain, let alone any view.

I could quote Wordsworth. He went up there and waxed lyrical about the extensive panorama, but you don't need to read Wordsworth to realize the truth of the matter. You just study the map. Obviously you must be able to see farther from Scafell Pike, but the highest peak in the country is in the middle of things and with so many mountain ranges hemming it in there must be some restriction in the continuity of the view. Not so with Black Combe. I am quite prepared to accept that in favourable conditions the mountains of North Wales are visible if you know what you are looking for and though you can see them from the Scafells too they must seem much more immediate with nothing but the sea to fill the space between. Black Combe is an outpost of the fell country and as an outpost it serves its purpose well.

When I stood at the foot of Black Combe and gazed at the wrapping of dark cloud swathing it from about 500 feet above my head I decided that this was an obvious invitation to try the trade route from Bootle to Whicham. In fact the map shows no right of way to allow a direct connection with Bootle but there is a link with the old bridleway that parallels the road above the intakes and this suggested a complete circuit which only coincides with the main road for a couple of hundred yards south of Whitebeck, so I parked in a layby south of the hamlet and started out. The concept was good, but after half a mile the idea of keeping to a set route began to pall and the desire to get off the beaten track drew me uphill. By the time I was opposite Stangrah I had explored the lower ravine of Miller Gill and was half-way across the next heathery buttress, level with the cloud ceiling. That was enough. I turned to face the slope and made straight for the summit.

The higher I climbed, the wetter it became. This was a straightforward, steady plod through springy heather, then grass, but the summit came sooner than expected as often is the case when you tackle a hill head-on. It was a surprise to reach the well-marked track across the plateau so quickly—it passes just below the top—and a few more steps brought the O.S. column into sight. The formalities had to be observed and out came the sandwiches, but it was only a token pause. With an icy spray in my face no matter how I used the windshelter there was no inclination to bring out the old mountain briar and in a few minutes I was back on the track and heading south.

Easy going, this, but a thousand feet below the mist had condescended to make a temporary clearance so I turned towards Townend Knotts for the conciliatory view over the Whicham Valley. It was sufficient to suggest that Black Combe's promise might be all that is claimed. I suppose this account is almost the story of non-event, just a minor adventure without the ultimate reward. But it had been a good afternoon despite the rain and I had seen enough to know that Black Combe must be worthy of its reputation as a magnificent viewpoint. I'll be back—but not unless I'm sure of the weather.

WHITESIDE PIKE

When the M6 was completed as a through route the old and time-honoured road over Shap became a piece of history for drivers of heavy goods vehicles. The ordinary motorist also tends to use the new motorway and the wild fells west of Shap seem even more remote from the bustle of modern life. Not many walkers ever did bother to look to these lonely hills and valleys for their recreation and on the few occasions when I have been in the area there has never been another walker in sight, just a few fell ponies, an occasional group of wide-ranging red deer—and of course the ubiquitous sheep that know these open spaces as their own personal preserve. Shap Fells are best known among fell walkers well versed in the topography of the district as the location of the other Borrowdale and the other Wasdale but for most folk these remain just names. This is not Lakeland, nor is there much to bring the best of Lakeland to mind until you reach as far west as the heads of Longsleddale, Mardale or Swindale. Yet there is one small summit on the edge of the Shap region that has the look of the real fell country and has a real cairn to prove it: Whiteside Pike. Here there is heather and bracken and the natural rock bursts through at the crest of the ridge to remind you of the favourite fells in the heart of the Lake District.

Whiteside Pike is quite prominent on the drive out of Kendal towards Shap. It is due north of the old market town and crowns the first rise of the ridge that separates Longsleddale from Bannisdale. The immediate surroundings are slaty in character—Bannisdale Slate—but the Coniston Grit outcrops at Whiteside Pike. It is obviously a more resistant rock for the Pike points a stubby finger at the sky as though to proclaim that here is something rather different from the general run of country hereabouts.

Bannisdale is virtually unknown, but Longsleddale has an appreciative and growing band of supporters though its road holds no encouragement for general tourism. It is five straight miles from the inconspicuous turning off the A6 to the limit of Longsleddale's metalled road at Sadgill but a traveller will cover rather more than this on a narrow lane which rarely conforms to the accepted notion of even an approximately straight line. Glacial in character, the valley is the last outpost of the typical fell country on this south-eastern fringe of the district. For the fell walker the best of Longsleddale is the final couple of miles above Sadgill where the ultimate reaches of the valley rise to Gatescarth Pass and the connection with Mardale. All that goes before is but a prelude.

The dale begins to take shape at Garnett Bridge, just off the A6. The lower valley is not deep but it is steeply sided in true glacial fashion. Though no lake is now present there is plentiful evidence to show that the wider parts held water in the distant past. Deciduous woodlands help to colour a pastoral land with a rich green in summer and at the close of the year the place glows in a riot of autumn hues. Always the River Sprint maintains its unifying thread through old lacustrine basins and short gorges on its way to join its cousin, the River Kent, a couple of miles north of Kendal. When you enter Longsleddale it is like taking a step back in time to a place where the old pele tower of Ubarrow Hall is a forgotten sentinel of days gone by.

If Longsleddale was forgotten, it is no more. This is a valley that has been rediscovered—but not so Bannisdale. Here is a dale that was never forgotten because it was never known in the first place and now it seems more deserted than ever. Lonely Bannisdale Head Farm wears a woebegone look in its ring of bleak hills. It is sad that such places can no longer support regular occupation, but how can remote farms like this justify their existence? Just thinking about the upkeep of the long supply road appalls. In fact the road slides into the valley from the side, less than a mile beyond the entry to Longsleddale. The little lane winds over the ridge, unsung and unnoticed, passing within a mile of the summit of Whiteside Pike. For a short distance this narrow road coincides with the original route over Shap, dating from a time when pack horses—and later coaches—made the crossing of Cumbria's eastern highlands. This makes even the superseded A6 a relative newcomer.

The easy way up Whiteside Pike starts here, though it is fair to say that a fell which is merely 1,302 feet in altitude cannot present much in the way of difficulty in ascent from any direction, apart from problems of access. The way past the farmstead of Moser is of outstanding simplicity along a rough lane that takes you within half a mile of the top. The total ascent cannot be more than 700 feet for, remember, you start high. You might think that it is hardly worth the effort but that would be a mistaken judgement. Here is one of those splendid miniature climbs that make an ideal break from routine if you are in the area with an hour or two to spare and just happen to have your boots with you. And in my case it would be most unusual for my boots to be absent for they live in my personal transport where they have their own individual niche. You never know!

The glory of Whiteside Pike is its summit. The real fells of Lakeland may be far away but here is one tiny sample which would not be out of place if dropped in the centre of the district. You can reach the crest by scrambling over rock if that is your pleasure and stepping up to the cairn is like stepping into the past. The top is not battle-scarred by boots or littered with orange peel and beer cans. The upstanding pyramid looks good from the A6 but when you stand at its apex the road is far enough away to be forgotten and the immediate surroundings are a mixture of rock, heather, bracken and grass with a few bright pools to mirror the sky. Who could wish for more?

Away to the east are the Howgills. The nicely proportioned hills of Whinfell Common fill the intermediate ground and a gorgeous greenery of pastures, walls and trees occupies the lowland spread between there and Kendal; and south of Kendal is a distant glimpse of sea—Morecambe Bay, of course. Nearer, you can see how the River Sprint carves its way out of Longsleddale. Almost below your feet is an appetizing scene where the farther flank of Longsleddale is lined with trees and the ravine of Dockernook Gill has an inviting look about it. Far away on the horizon is a tantalizing peep of the Scafells. Perhaps the best-looking hills in the panorama are the neat cones of Ill Bell and Froswick at the other side of Kentmere with whole ranges of mountains backing them up in splendid array. To the north is contrast. From here the trench of Bannisdale looks bleak and uninviting, an impression heightened by the rather dreary expanse of the Shap Fells in the background.

Bannisdale is not really as unattractive as I make it sound. When I climbed Whiteside Pike I continued along the ridge to Grey Crag near the head of Longsleddale and returned down Bannisdale. It is a pleasant enough valley in a quiet sort of way. Simple slopes of rough, tussocky grass seal the dale at its head but Bannisdale Beck tumbles noisily out of such unpromising beginnings and I remember one waterslide amid the cascades where the beck pours in a subdued rush over a wide bar of rock that seeks to block its course. Evening shadows were filling the dale as I passed through the old farmyard of Bannisdale Head, and for a moment I was disturbed by the sight of a stationary watcher on the skyline to the right—but it was only the tall cairn on Black Crag.

There is a peculiar unreality about walking down a long, empty valley at dusk. The silence was almost complete. The sound of water is so integral a part of the Lake Country that it can pass unnoticed, but there were occasional bird calls to provide company. Near Dryhowe Bridge I paused to watch the moon, revealed by a break in drifting clouds so that gnarled bare hawthorns seemed to reach out with black silhouettes of jagged boughs. A robin flew up with a nervous "tic" and a moth brushed my face as it fluttered uncertainly across the track. Not far away an owl called. It was the last day in October—Hallowe'en. A timid mortal could be in trouble here, I thought, reassuring myself that all was well. But I moved on just the same.

It had been a quiet afternoon in the solitude of lonely hills with only the wind and birds as company. I would say that not another human being was seen during the entire walk, but it would not be strictly true. Near Grey Crag a couple of jet aircraft in close partnership crossed the ridge barely a hundred feet above my head, near enough for the pilots to be visible in the brief but violent seconds of their passing. It was the only jarring moment in an otherwise peaceful day.

SOUTHER FELL

Let's get the name right for a start. It's spelled Souther with a "th" in the middle but you pronounce it with a hard "t", just like the Italians have pronounced it in Othello ever since Verdi adapted Shakespeare for the operatic stage: "Souter" Fell. Having got that out of my system, perhaps we can get on with it.

Souther Fell is the first hill in Lakeland as you drive in from Penrith along the A66. But it is by no means the first hill you notice for it is completely overshadowed by the dominating shape of Blencathra which shows the high, distinctive form that gained it a second, and for a long time more popular name, Saddlcback. The ancient title is once more enjoying a vogue but it is plain to see why "Saddle-back" had its adherents for so long a time when you look at it from this eastern viewpoint. It is also easy to understand why Souther Fell is almost forgotten for it is in every way subservient to its higher, more massive and infinitely more dramatic parent. After all, it is really no more than a grassy extension of Blencathra's east ridge and not many walkers consider Souther Fell worthy of an ascent for itself. You may safely assume that most visitors to its gentle ridge-top are prompted by a vague curiosity. They want to see what is there, they have heard stories of a famous legend, maybe they wish to add it to their bag of "Wainwrights", but usually it is treated as an extra on an ascent of the major fell. If Blencathra was not there they would be walking elsewhere.

This is the fate of Souther Fell, a genuine foothill which must for ever bow to the superior claims of one of Lakeland's major mountains. And yet Souther Fell is not without interest—but it is interesting for reasons of geographical curiosity and as a setting for a Lake District legend rather than for any intrinsic excitement. If you climb Souther Fell in search of a bit of typical Lakeland fell country you will be sadly disappointed. Turn away, friend, and look elsewhere—or go on to climb Blencathra. Souther Fell is not for you.

The fell takes the shape of a modest whale-back of a ridge with no subsidiaries. Apart from a rash of stones on the western flank all is grass and a little bracken, the sort of hill to make sheep bleat with joy. But on the right day and in the right frame of mind you can have an enjoyable little excursion on Souther Fell.

Its position on the north-eastern margin of the district allows a wide view across the vale of Eden with the Pennines as a distant horizon, and from the northern end of the ridge a more intimate scene catches the eye. The best ascent is made from this end with the hamlet of Mungrisdale as the starting point and as you climb there is a retrospective view of the little group of buildings, a scene of homely charm. Once you are on top it is inevitably Blencathra that takes command, though in the early stages you have Bannerdale Crags and Bowscale Fell competing for attention.

A geographical curiosity of Souther Fell is very apparent from the map. It is almost completely surrounded by just one river, the Glenderamackin. Only where it abuts Blencathra is the encirclement broken, almost a moated mountain you might say—if it had the height and character to be a mountain. At the col above Mousthwaite Combe the Glenderamackin almost manages to short-circuit the wide loop to the north but a couple of hundred feet of rising ground effectively diverts the stream and maintains the watershed. The beck—it is hardly a river at this stage—must take the long way round through the village of Mungrisdale before it is eventually able to journey west and join the waters of central Lakeland on their way to the Irish Sea.

My daughter has a music book with a picture of a smooth green hill with a long line of tiny figures climbing the skyline to the summit, the Grand Old Duke of York and his 10,000 men. When I look at it I think of Souther Fell, not because of the Duke of York but because of the legend that brings unsought fame to the quiet little hill. There are stories of ghostly occurrences on the grassy slopes, some of which may well be relegated to the realms of local folklore, but one event has the backing of respectable evidence. This most reported example was in the summer of 1745 when local residents were willing to swear in the presence of a magistrate that they had seen an army on the fell, hundreds of tiny figures on the march in black silhouette against the late evening sky.

This was on Midsummer Eve, in common with similar reports of earlier years, which would lend credibility to suggestions that it was an unearthly manifestation. In days of yore Midsummer Eve was regarded in the same superstitious awe as Hallowe'en as an occasion for supernatural events; yet when some two dozen known and respected local citizens were prepared to take an oath as testimony to the truth of this strange army there seemed good reason to investigate the matter further—but not before the light of Midsummer Day when Souther Fell appeared as deserted as it normally is. So large a body of men would surely leave some mark of its passing but no

sign of any presence was to be found, nor any large encampment in the valley beyond. It was all very strange.

There is a theory that it was a trick of refracted light for
it became known that Prince Charles's rebel army was on
the move in southern Scotland at precisely the same time.
Was it a mirage? Or was it something else? Some authorities affirm that the Old British name of nearby
Blencathra means "The Hill of Devils", though it is little
more than a guess. The only sure thing is that "Blen"
means hill. The rest is lost in obscurity, but if memories of
supposed devils do have some connection with this unusual, musically sonorous collection of letters then perhaps visions of a similar nature to that of Midsummer Eve,
1745, have been noted on these hills since before the time
of recorded history.

You may believe in the ghosts of Souther Fell or not, but
the story adds a touch of colour to a rather ordinary hill.
The only unlikely event I have witnessed there concerned
the apparently gymnastic ability of a horse. I was passing
a roadside barn near Scales, on the lane that runs round
the base of the fell to Mungrisdale, when I glanced up-
wards and saw a horse's head peering down at me from the
roof-tree. The possibility of cross-breeding with a giraffe
seemed highly improbable, hardly less so than the idea
that horses might fly. The obvious truth was that the level
of pasture behind the barn was higher than the road in
front. It was an excellent opportunity for a gimmicky
photograph but I was too slow. Pegasus ambled away and
could not be enticed to return.

When I took Sarah over Souther Fell there were no
magical horses straight out of the fairy tales and no spec-
tral army on manoeuvres along the grassy top. You don't
even get armies of fell walkers up there. We did see a
couple of walkers at the summit and a small mountain
tent was pitched on Mousthwaite Col. As far as Souther
Fell is concerned a total of four visitors at one time and a
nearby encampment of a single tiny tent constitutes a
crowd. If you are looking for peace and quiet on August
Bank Holiday Monday, then Souther Fell is as good a place
to be as any.

BINSEY

The A591 road sweeps into Lakeland between the tree-decked skirts of Skiddaw and the shy waters of Bassen-thwaite Lake. An aspirant fell walker approaching the district from this unusual angle sees a strange view of England's fourth-highest mountain and a pleasing panorama of the hinterland of Newlands, a region full of opportunity for striding high ridges in a well-endowed section of the Cumbrian fells. This busy road has had its corners smoothed—in common with many a Lakeland highway—and the tiny hamlet of Bewaldeth is now happily separated from the thoroughfare. East of the road, just after you enter the National Park, is a gentle hill that must rarely attract a glance from travellers speeding towards Keswick. Binsey has always enjoyed a position of isolation but this lonely outlier has its own ancient history and can provide a few hours of easy wandering nicely off the beaten track. I have known it spring one or two surprises to enliven a quiet afternoon away from the jostle of the popular places. But when I found myself face to face with a bull in one of Binsey's pastures the old fellow seemed too bored to take notice, I'm pleased to say. Perhaps prolonged acquaintance with Binsey in all weathers does have that effect on you.

A casual glance suggests little to bring walkers to Binsey. You see a smooth sort of mound, a precursor of the main group of fells north of Keswick you might reasonably suppose, but don't let this unassuming appearance fool you. The hill differs from its neighbours in one important respect so that it has more in common with the mighty Scafell Pike than nearby Skiddaw, for all the apparent similarity. Binsey is a fell of the Borrowdale Volcanic series. Here amongst the slate is an exposure of the stuff of which the real mountains are made—though it is hardly diplomatic to suggest that Skiddaw is not a real mountain, slate or not. It is true, however, that the hallmark of the typical Lake District scene is the dramatic crags and splendid tarns to be found in association with the volcanic rocks.

There are no great crags on Binsey but the right kind of

rock is there all right. As if to underline the point the hill overlooks one of the district's biggest tarns in an area where any tarn at all is a rarity. You don't find many tarns on slate. Yet a visitor stirred into exploratory activity by this suggestion of exciting rock sculpture is bound to come away with a sense of disappointment. Prior study of the one-inch Tourist Map could have saved him a journey. The smooth plan of evenly spaced contours is not broken by the hachures that the Ordnance Surveyors use to denote crags and outcrops, which only goes to show that Binsey is true to its appearance from the main road. There is a small cliff, West Crag, above Bewaldeth but it is nothing to write home about. You would pass it without a turn of the head if it stood beside the track out of Wasdale.

The basic rock of the fell is most evident on the summit. You can hardly miss it. The O.S. map gives an enigmatic clue to the nature of this rock-littered crest, though the single word "tumulus" adds to the mystery rather than solves it. Was it an ancient British burial site, or a well-marked look-out point? Maybe the question can never be answered but it matters little to most of today's visitors who have built a small collection of windshelters from this handy open quarry. No doubt the O.S. column originated in the stones of the tumulus too. Possibly the spot had religious associations for the ancients but there is nothing sacred about it as far as modern man is concerned.

I first went up there in the early sixties, a gentle stroll in the late afternoon costing little in effort but encouraging a healthy appetite for the evening meal. I came round from the north where tiny villages still seem to escape the blatant tourism of central Lakeland. Ireby and High Ireby rest in a pleasantly rural setting and Ruthwaite enjoys a minor fame as the one-time home of John Peel but it is much less a target for tourist pilgrims than the celebrated huntsman's grave at Caldbeck.

Half a dozen years ago we climbed Binsey on an overcast day when the likelihood of cold drizzle made the higher fells an unpleasant prospect for a family outing. When we reached it low cloud drifted across the summit and we were glad to make use of the most substantial of those windbreaks. Mist swirled around, doing its best to seal us from the larger world and the view, but occasional breaks allowed us the privilege of a fleeting panorama.

Away to the south-east, nestling in the shadow of bulky Skiddaw, the secluded valley of Dash Beck points directly at Binsey. On a day of sunshine the well-named falls of Whitewater Dash show up splendidly. Strangely, they can seem more conspicuous from here than from the track to Skiddaw House only a hundred yards from the cataract. Naturally enough Skiddaw looms large in the view and the land of ridges at the far side of Bass Lake shows an interesting display from this unusual angle. The lake also looks good, directing a watery finger to the heart of Lakeland. Turn your back on the hills—if only for a moment—and there is the Solway Plain. It may lack the excitement of the high fells but there is plenty to see in that direction, especially if you spread out the map and identify the landmarks. Much nearer are two little tarns, only half a mile away, that have become conspicuous with the clearance of trees in the nearest enclosures of Binsey's northern flank.

Just a year previously Binsey's modest pate had a cap of snow in June—it was two feet deep on Skiddaw—and now we watched a squall of rain heading our way and felt that it was cold enough for snow again. Certainly the weather was doing little to encourage a long stay. On a good June day we might have lounged about for an hour but this time we were soon on our feet to turn in the general direction of Ireby, down the acres of heather that adorn the upper northern flank.

We had gone some 400 yards when a lithe red form sprang out of the ling only a couple of dozen strides ahead. Probably we had been in Reynard's sights almost since we had left the summit but the fox had decided that we presented no threat. Now that we were obviously on a collision course it was time for him to do something about it. He was in view for a second or so and if I had not been looking that way I would have known nothing of his presence. A single leap over one obstacle was traced by his graceful brush, then he was gone. My wife and Sarah, whose eyes were elsewhere, missed him altogether though I was quick to point him out.

This encounter was typical of a neighbourhood which is in quiet contrast with the busy A591 to the south, though even there you don't see many strangers in the rural backwater away from the road. You can walk the leafy lanes behind Binsey in peace and there is every chance of observing the wildlife of the countryside. A couple of years ago we disturbed a hunting stoat as it prospected along the verge. With a black flick from the tip of its tail it vanished into the long grass. Earlier we had put up a startled hare which had disappeared with equal speed. Even the songs of the birds seem fuller and more contented among the quiet byways of Ireby.

14

THE SOFT CENTRE
(A Walk on the Wet Side, West of Thirlmere)

If you ask the average fell walker to name the most central fell of all you will probably hear High Raise mentioned—or, if your informant prefers the alternative title, High White Stones. Others with a leaning towards pedantic accuracy may choose Armboth Fell, but really a reasonable case could be made out for any top between these points. It all depends upon where you place the boundaries of the Lake District fells and that is very much a personal matter. Certainly the area of high ground between Borrowdale and Thirlmere, reaching from Langdale in the south to Keswick in the north, deserves to be called the Central Fells. Wainwright settles for that label and there is no adequate reason to question his judgement. The highest land in the group is in the southern half with High Raise the most elevated point so on that count it may reasonably be accepted as the most central fell.

This highest section stretches as far north as Ullscarf beyond which there is no 2,000-foot contour, though High Seat comes within about five feet of being a 2,000 footer. The wide, peaty ridge centred upon High Seat is bounded by some of the busiest valleys in the district and some of the little fells on its western fringe attract visitors in great numbers. When we used to camp near Castlerigg the pre-breakfast stroll to the top of Walla Crag was almost a statutory requirement and the state of the track is ample testimony to its popularity as a viewpoint—but the watershed of the ridge can be a place of solitude. Unless you go there in dry weather it is easy to understand why. A wide top where there is a minimum of gradient until you reach the flanking slopes is not the sort of place to facilitate quick drainage and the acres of peat soak up the rain and release it with reluctance so that there is more in common with the Featherbed Mosses of the southern Pennines than with the typical Lakeland fell country.

I remember a short walk from Keswick to Watendlath when we kept well to the west of the central ridge, enjoying views from the tops of Walla Crag and Falcon Crag before we turned away from the Borrowdale edge. I don't suppose we came within half a mile of the top of High Seat before we turned due south, and at Raise Gill we scrambled down to Watendlath and its tarn. It was a fine day with the sun in our faces and I have no doubt that the outlook over Derwentwater and the Borrowdale scene was as good as it always is, but I don't recall it. I *do* remember the constant squelch as boots sank into soft, soggy ground during the latter half of the walk. From that moment I decided that the only time to visit the soft centre of the English Lake District would be in a period of extended drought or when the frosts of winter seal the water into the spongy peat.

These moderate fells have a Reputation—the capital letter is intended—but they are by no means as bad they are painted. I have traversed much worse bogs in the southern Pennines in an area where this sort of thing is taken for granted. However in Lakeland, where you have a superabundance of really attractive fells at your disposal, this relatively low-lying and comparatively dull piece of upland is not everyone's choice and it has become fashionable to regard it as wet to the point of exaggeration. You might expect the area to be a trackless wilderness but such is not the case. Long-established tracks cross from Watendlath to Armboth and Wythburn and a track along the watershed has become established with the passing years, showing that the plateau is by no means shunned. It could be that the Reputation is an attraction and walkers feel that their Lakeland education is not complete until they can boast of experiences in the watery waste.

The east and west flanks of the upland plateau could hardly be more different. There is a lake at either side but there the resemblance ends. Derwentwater is a lake, one of the best. Thirlmere was a lake but it became a reservoir

and though Manchester's supervision is more enlightened
nowadays, to the point of providing forest trails and in-
formation, the dale remains a captive valley. In Borrowdale you feel free—even the little plantations of Great
Wood below Walla Crag seem less an infringement upon
personal liberty than the blanket tree-scape around Thirlmere. The road to the west of Thirlmere provides a pleasant drive, an attractive alternative to the busy A591 for
motorists not in any hurry, and there are some good,
long-ranging vistas over the water, but this is tourist
country. The walker is at a disadvantage. There *are* points
where there is access to the fells, it is true, but they need
seeking out. When compared with the life and gaiety of the
bustling crowds below the Borrowdale slopes the Thirlmere side seems under the spell of an anaesthetic.

West of Thirlmere dyed-in-the-wool fell walkers are
thin on the ground. Of course the other side of the reservoir
has its popular routes to Helvellyn, over Sticks Pass and
even to the Dods but that is a different story. You soon
climb above the trees and there is plenty of open fell to
attract walkers looking to reach the highest continuous
ridge in the district, indeed it is rare that those tracks are
empty of traffic even though the better side of Helvellyn
and its satellites faces Ullswater. West of Thirlmere the
only routes in anything like regular use are those that
connect with Watendlath.

There is only one minor fell which enjoys even modest
popularity—Raven Crag—and that is as much a rock
climbers' crag as a place for walkers, and even then the
only real resemblance to genuine fell walking is the steepness of the ascent. You tend to feel that something is
missing when you climb amongst trees. But the effort is
worthwhile if you choose the right day. As a viewpoint the
top of Raven Crag is in a class of its own, a platform on the
edge of space with the verticality of the crag uncom-
fortably close and vast beds of bilberry uncropped by sheep
so that there is a rich feast awaiting walkers when the
fruit is in season. You can always recognize those who
have reached the summit by studying the colour of their
fingers.

We took Sarah up Raven Crag on a rather damp afternoon when further rain was obviously imminent. As it happened we had completed this short walk and were taking off our boots when the clouds decided to release their burden—good timing because, whatever her views about walking, young Sarah has quite definite opinions on one subject. She does not approve of getting wet. Climbs amid plantations always seem to me rather less arduous than they appear in prospect, which is strange because the vertical lines of the conifers show the angle of slope in no uncertain terms. But maybe therein lies the secret. The soaring shafts of evergreen betray the mountainside and the true angle of gradient is never as sharp as appearances suggest. The forest rides are a help too, as are way-marked footpaths. If you get away from the beaten track it is a different story. There is nothing easy about direct ascents in virgin forest.

Overlooking Shoulthwaite Gill on the west of Raven Crag is the hill-fort site of Castle Crag, though its interest is more a matter for imagination than observation. All the same it is worth a visit if only for the variety engendered by a bare rocky knoll free of all those trees. A nearby forestry observation tower creates more excitement as far as adventurous youngsters are concerned—and at least one member of an older generation has experienced the urge to climb the widely spaced rungs to the platform.

Shoulthwaite Gill is one of the quieter spots in Lakeland but it is an exciting little valley enlivened by a sparkling, bouncing beck set between steep slopes with plantations on one side and a bare fellside and crags on the other. The crags—Goat Crag and Iron Crag—are steep places, steep enough and high enough to bring a speculative gleam to the eye of the rock climber. Iron Crag appears to overhang, at least the lower rampart does. A few years ago when walking into the northern fells "back of' Skidda'" I looked back and saw this little cliff display its outline to good effect as a bank of cloud settled behind it. The sun was shining as I stood above the Glenderaterra Beck but there was rain sweeping across central Lakeland and the background of a vigorous squall in Shoulthwaite Gill gave Iron

Crag a dramatic, gravity-defying silhouette. The overall effect was oddly reminiscent of some old sepia prints of the district with pearly mist creeping round Naddle Fell and the upper reaches of Shoulthwaite Gill bathed in a vaporous opalescence.

A couple of years later—it was that glorious summer of 1976 when the sun shone for months on end and the fells dried like tinder—I walked into the Shoulthwaite valley before indulging in an afternoon saunter over its hinterland. Week after week the sun had been at work desiccating the central morass, becks were reduced to a trickle and some of the tinier tarns had gone into hibernation. The government had taken the unprecedented step of appointing a minister for drought and the country was gradually drying up in the grip of one of the greatest droughts in living memory. A month earlier I had wandered through upper Eskdale to reach the summit of England through the lonely wilderness of Little Narrowcove and even then there was hardly a drop of water to be seen above the River Esk. Little Narrowcove was fast turning into a desert and I reached the cairn of Scafell Pike wilting like a lettuce leaf in an oven. There seemed little doubt that the watershed between Thirlmere and Borrowdale would be drier than for many a long year and as the weeks passed I began to realize that I was missing an opportunity so rarely granted.

Five weeks after the day on the Scafells my wife dropped me at Dale Bottom and drove off to do some shopping, the arrangement being to meet me at the foot of Launchy Gill four hours later. There would be plenty of time for what I had in mind and time enough for a little off-beat exploration too, if I had the mind for it. First I strolled up to little Snipes How Tarn to see if it was still there. It was not; just a green area ringed by grey stones. Already the perspiration was flowing but I could hardly remove any more clothes. The staple wear that summer was shorts, socks and boots, but I saw no one on the fells until High Seat so lack of modesty would have gone unnoticed—but there are limits! The outstanding memory of this early part of the climb above Snipes How was of bracken but the name on the map should have been a warning: Bracken Riggs. The flourishing fronds were in prime condition, tough and rasping, sawing away at my calves and making their presence felt at every step. In this sort of terrain you pay the penalty for wearing shorts but I had made my choice and there was no alternative but to stick to it. Bracken seems to thrive in any conditions, it never seems unhealthy and there is little wonder that the hill farmer regards it as an unmitigated pest.

I scrambled up to Goat Crag where platforms of smooth grass sheltered by the cliff simmered in the afternoon heat, a peaceful spot. The pleasant strath of Shoulthwaite Gill reached into the interior in lonely contrast to the bustle beside Naddle Beck. A couple of forestry workmen were busy near the stream, far below. The rhythmic "chunk-chunk" of an axe and the muffled drone of a chainsaw in the plantation; these were the only sounds apart from the subdued traffic noise on the A591. The spasmodic activities of the woodsmen brought the solitude of central Lakeland into sharper focus and I paused for a moment, enjoying the freedom of the fells.

The final approach to the summit of Bleaberry Fell should have included acquaintance with the first swamp but it was virtually dry. The heathery top is triple cairned and, despite being set well back from the surrounding valleys, it is a good viewpoint. There is a sense of airy spaciousness about the place on a day of clear skies and sunshine and there was no doubt that I was seeing it at its best. North of the summit the ground falls to a considerable tilted step where tussocky grass introduces a dreary aspect to the immediate foreground, but it hardly impinges on the senses because it is below eye-level. You look beyond all this, across the Greta valley to the wide façade of the northern fells with an impressive build-up of the Skiddaw group on the left and Blencathra's formidable frontage of ridges and ravines away to the right. I turned about to face south, settled beside the cairn with a sandwich in my hand and considered the question of the moment. Would it be wet or dry?

Well—mainly dry. I crossed areas that are obviously

swamp in their normal state and remained dry-shod where it would never do to pause and look around in the average summer. Considering the ill-repute of this ridge it was surprising to find the track so well defined—and there was more than one track. Perhaps the good weather had brought an influx of folk anxious to test the route in these optimum conditions, or maybe the route is well trodden because of necessity it follows the driest line. Now it stood out plain to see, a rich black scar in the peat always visible ahead as it wove a serpentine course around grass knolls and miniature peat-moss tarns—and with more direct alternatives making temporary crossings of the dry beds of former pools.

There were four walkers on High Seat and a party of Scouts had just departed. On High Tove I met a couple crossing the ridge. They complained that they had been unable to find Armboth—the village—which was hardly surprising, though the low level of Thirlmere meant that much of the old valley was temporarily in view, with field patterns of tumbled walls showing on the parched bed of the reservoir.

I made a bee-line for Armboth Fell walking where no sane person would usually venture and continued to Launchy Gill to find that Launchy Tarn had retained its identity on this arid hinterland. Plunging boldly down steep banks into the plantations I succumbed to temptation and enjoyed a brief, cool dip in an enticing rock pool— a delicious conclusion to a grand walk in country completely foreign to its normal self. And the rendezvous with transport was made precisely on time. Who could ask for more?

15

FOUR FOR THE CONNOISSEUR
(Silver How; Place Fell; Grange Fell; Haystacks)

Which is your favourite fell? Obviously this is a question that every man (or woman—let's have no sex discrimination here!) can answer only for himself. It is a favourite game of mine, and my friends, to sort out the fells and choose a personal top ten and though the final selection is almost invariably the same the act of selection is always a pleasant way of passing the odd hour when we have nothing better to do. Often we would drive home after a day in the hills and discuss the respective merits of various fells and try to arrive at a reasonable short-list of candidates to put forward for top position. Sometimes by way of variety we would choose our best tarns or supreme mountain passes, or sometimes it would simply be our favourite place to be in the fells, but I suppose the real object of the exercise was to allow us a little reminiscence about our favourite leisure activity and to extend our day on the fells as long as possible as we drove home to face a workaday world on the morrow.

In one of his books A. Wainwright tells us that his favourite fell is the one that he happens to be on at the time and that is as good an answer as any, but if you don't happen to be on a fell when the problem is posed it is not a really satisfactory reply. Yet it remains an excellent way of avoiding the traumas of an impossible decision, of avoiding being pinned down to a personal choice when there are so many variables and such a magnificent list at your disposal. Perhaps I could put it this way: if you were to be granted one last fell to climb, which would you choose? Oh! what an agony of decision and indecision that hypothetical query would pose! At least for the purposes of this book we can discount the major fells—major in terms of height, that is to say.

When I sketched out a provisional plan for the book I had this chapter in mind from the outset. Though originally I set a height limit of 2,000 feet the final choice includes one slightly higher than this, but its summit is less than 1,700 feet above the valley so a secondary criterion allows it to qualify for inclusion: in no instance is there an ascent of 2,000 feet. The short list included Loughrigg, Catbells, Causey Pike, Mellbreak, Stickle Pike and Helm Crag so these would complete a provisional top ten, but the list is fluid. Yet I see no reason to change the quartet that contest the top spot. They are not arranged in ascending order, rather in a geographical, anticlockwise spiral, but the starting point is such as will allow Haystacks the final position. This is deliberate. In the opinion of many a walker this gem of a fell is the finest of the smaller hills, only lack of height depriving it of the supreme position in a comprehensive list of all Lakeland's mountains—but if it did happen to be higher many of its qualities would suffer; however, more of that when the moment to discuss its merits arrives. Suffice to say that in a poll of merit there is every reason to suppose that Haystacks would take the prime position amongst foothills and I would certainly place it there. The other three would surely take high places. I wonder how many of you will agree with my choice?

SILVER HOW

Silver How must surely be an established favourite with many a connoisseur of the hills. Although very much a minor fell, just 1,292 feet in height and undistinguished in outline, it holds a beauty quite in keeping with the attractive name. No one who sets foot on its delectable acres ever comes away disappointed. It fits neatly into the pattern of heights that help Great Langdale's lower valley to take shape. Certain characteristics are shared with immediate neighbours, Loughrigg and Blea Rigg, while across the dale is Lingmoor—perhaps the most shapely member of this quartet.

From Langdale Silver How is an unexceptional slope of rough fell, unnoticed by travellers who have eyes only for the exciting display of the famous Pikes and major mountains that dominate the head of the dale. For this reason, at least, Silver How must be considered as a Grasmere fell. Even from Grasmere there is little about the outline to fix it in the memory. Helm Crag with its Lion and its Lamb is the one that commands attention from Wordsworth's fair vale, rather than the knobbly bank of rising land due west of the lake. However, there is much more to Silver How than a casual glance suggests. It is full of those features that make walking a pleasurable occupation for the family, as well as providing interesting ground for the dedicated fell walker's off-day.

The western boundary is not easily defined. A wide ridge merges indefinitely with Blea Rigg but I like to think of Lang How and its tiny tarns as part of Silver How, for an exploration of the area is incomplete if their charms remain unsampled. The eastern limits are more positively marked. The fell throws a protective arm around the south-western shore of the lake, above which is the well-known low pass of Red Bank. Here is the short, steep road that connects Grasmere with Elterwater, not a happy place for motorists in high season. It is certainly a dangerous place for foot travellers, though evasive action can be taken by using the way through Deerbolts Wood.

Silver How has a modest footing in Easedale where it helps Helm Crag to form the gateway to a popular valley. Here, on the lowest slopes below the open fell is Allan Bank, for a short time the home of Wordsworth. The poet spent only three years of his long life at this house—he found the place draughty and moved on as soon as an opportunity allowed—but his stay at Allan Bank gave the fell its most certain claim to literary associations. An ascent of Silver How is one of the most rewarding of gentler outings from Grasmere and the way through the grounds of Allan Bank allows views into the portals of Easedale that are really delightful. Trees make the scene in what is one of Lakeland's most exquisite displays. It is difficult to select the lovelier season—spring or autumn—

but it would be hard to better the leafy pyrotechnics at the close of the year when a riotous explosion of colour is breathtaking in its effect. The early morning, with wisps of mist rising from the trees and melting in the sharp, fresh air, that is a time of special magic.

Beyond the final walls is the only bit of steepness but with such a wealth of beauty on all sides it is hardly noticed. There is no desire to hurry in such surroundings and a cairn at the top of the sharpest rise encourages a pause to take in the retrospective panorama. Even in the busiest season the sylvan setting hides the bustle of Grasmere and makes the village look at peace with the world though you may not think so if you happen to be down there. The track wends a lazy way through patches of juniper. Some of these wind-blown little trees are delightful examples of natural sculpture. It would seem that an expert in topiary has been busy through the ages, trimming silhouettes of fantastic fascination, and down on the right is a minor gill richly clothed in warm evergreen shades. Soon a small cairn indicates a division of ways—left to Silver How direct, right by way of Lang How.

The latter is the way for me. It contours round varied humps and on the left is lower ground with Silver How's summit beyond. This is the gathering ground of Wray Gill with the tiny stream wending its way towards the steeper plunge to the lake. At one point a placid meander cuts a miniature gorge through a mound of boulder clay, but every little feature of this landscape is a delight to the eye. You can continue round Lang How and look at the little tarn that figures as foreground in many a photograph of the Langdale Pikes. Lang How Tarn, or Silver How Tarn if you prefer—it has a number of names and W. Heaton Cooper also suggests Youdell Tarn, Yewcrag Tarn and Robin Tarn in his superb book, *The Tarns of Lakeland*—this pool seems to be a healthy breeding ground for reeds. Choose your season to see it at its best, but with its views of the Langdale fells and valley it is always a good place to visit.

If there was no more to Silver How than this ascent from Grasmere the fell would still merit a high place in my top

ten foothills, but there are other attractive ways just waiting to be found. I remember reaching the summit from the
Red Bank road, crossing the eastern slopes from the narrow walled lane near the boat landings. As a popular
walkers' route to Langdale it has to withstand a fair
amount of traffic and it can be rather muddy in places, but
it still has charm with intimate views of Grasmere and
Loughrigg opening up as you climb. You can head back to
the summit when the watershed is reached, or take a short
cut up a scree rake from the last corner of the wall. The
former route is gentler on the feet but those screes are not
without interest. The enigmatic sound of running water is
heard where none is visible. Silver How's hidden stream
trickles shyly beneath the stones.

The scree route takes you to the foot of the small crag
that defends the summit on the east. We have opened our
sandwiches above these rocks, out of sight of the top
though only a few steps from the busy promenade. Here
is seclusion and relative comfort, an airy perch with
Grasmere spread out like a corner of paradise. One
September morning the lake sparkled with twinkling
highlights in the wake of a solitary boat and swallows
dived and soared at our feet in quest of insects. One eccentric flight followed a wavering butterfly along the crest
of the little crag as sheep stretched lazily in the grass
below.

A pool on the ridge to Loughrigg caught the light and led
the eye to Loughrigg Tarn. Farther afield a reach of Windermere competed for attention, while to the south we
were pleased to recognize a tiny glimpse of Coniston
Water. Loughrigg seems quite unexceptional from here
yet it is such a happy fell, the scene of many a memorable
ramble and a firm favourite with those who know it inti-
mately. Ambleside's gasholder peeps incongruously above
the outline but much, much farther away is the faint shape
of Ingleborough, a reminder of more strenuous days in the
Yorkshire Dales. Farthest of Lakeland's fells in view is
Blencathra, due north, seen through the window of
Dunmail Raise with Helvellyn on the right.

But pride of place in this outlook does not belong to the

heights. Grasmere is the centre-piece. It is truly a village of trees set in surroundings of shapely hills and with the sun in the heavens there is the lambent glow of its own personal lake to bring it all to life. From this summit it is obvious that Silver How is Grasmere's fell. Who could deny so charming a village the patronage of this most exquisite of smaller hills?

PLACE FELL

A score of years ago I took a young cousin on his first Lakeland walk. We reached no summit as we walked from Grasmere to Patterdale on a day when Grisedale Hause was a place of mists and—especially for a teenage lad new to the hills—a place of mystery too. From the hause we dropped towards the tarn, where wavelets rippling along the shore were heard before any water was seen, and then began the descent to Grisedale. Only seconds later we were beneath the ceiling of cloud and a golden valley stretched before us. There was sun on this side of the watershed, piercing the clouds with shafts of light and colouring the slopes on either hand. But as we came down into Grisedale the main spotlight picked out an eye-catching fell far ahead. We walked the long strath with this challenging shape always before us, its challenge being in a rugged western face rather than in any inspiring outline: Place Fell.

At the time Place Fell was an undiscovered hill as far as I was concerned but from that moment it had to find a slot in my itinerary, as surely it must for anyone who has seen it and has taken the time to study it from across Ullswater's upper reach. This is the finest side of the fell, a two-mile sweep of crag, scree, heather and juniper plunging more than a thousand feet from the skyline to the water's edge. The varied colours, particularly late in the day before the sun sets behind Helvellyn, must be seen to be believed. Old mine and quarry workings are to be found if you know where to look but the passage of time and the healing hand of nature have done much to obliterate the scars. And beside the lake, sometimes at the foot of the fell, sometimes climbing a considerable way up the slope, is a delectable track that is possibly the finest waterside walk in the British Isles. Here is the very essence of Ullswater's glorious scene, a distillation of all that is best in Lakeland.

A feature of the walk is the constant unfolding of vistas which display new reaches of the lake, sometimes from near the shore, sometimes well above. Names on the map help paint a picture of fairyland charm: Silver Hill, Silver Crag, Silver Point and Silver Bay hold out a promise that is entirely fulfilled. There are stands of trees framing views that linger in the memory, patches of grass like lawns in a landscaped garden, and bays and beaches along the shore are tailor-made for unhurried picnic parties. When one more headland is rounded and the head of the lake still fails to appear it would seem that Ullswater goes on for ever and I doubt if I am alone in wishing this was true. They say you can find glow-worms on this flank of Place Fell, if you know where to look. The idea of these creatures illuminating the summer nights represents for me a romance fully in keeping with the charms of so beautiful a setting.

Between Silver Point and Patterdale the fellside is at its steepest. There was an evening climb on this flank when I reached the summit as the sun slid behind the Helvellyn Dods. The happy cries of children playing by the water faded until an easing of the contours shut them off as abruptly as the turning of a knob on the radio. The mood of the fell changed too. More grass, less rock, a stillness in the air and a kestrel hovering against the palely glowing blue of the sky brought a spice of solitude. Near the top the shadows of the valley were reaching up to claim the fell for the night but I still had rays of weakening sunshine to light the way to the cairn, and as I rested for a few minutes beside the highest rocks a cold and penetrating breeze swept in from the distant Pennines.

Another day—and this same fellside holds different memories. This was a family outing with a hot sun on our backs. A school party at the summit shared the top of the fell with other happy folk going their separate ways. The mood of the day was completely different from the peace of my evening jaunt but even so, between the lakeside track and the wide top, we saw no one. Yet the fellside still had nothing in common with the loneliness of late evening. In place of the kestrel there was a cuckoo whose call erupted from a patch of scrub a dozen or so yards from where we sat. It took flight—so near we could almost count its individual feathers—and floated down to the trees of Blawick where it resumed its interrupted call.

You can wander here and feel yourself a pioneer but the steep slope is not without tracks. Some of them become more marked with the passing years as discerning walkers look for less trodden ways but a grassy carpet still softens the footfall and butterwort does not have to fight for existence along moist, steeper sections. I went up there very early one morning and watched the world awaken. The lake, still and shadowed, was a mirror to tiny puffs of cumulus drifting like candy-floss across a cold blue sky and the cool air of night still clung to the steep hillside. Birdsong filled the opening hours of a new day. A few yards away a wren was loud in its territorial claims as it darted among the junipers. I perched on a rock and tried to locate it and caught a few fleeting glimpses—very few and very fleeting, though one of its stations was only a couple of yards from my boots in the deep shade of wind-flattened bushes.

An hour passed, and more. The sun topped the hill behind me and filled the valley with its golden glow as one by one the folk down there came out to go about their business. In a camp site by the water the tents began to show evidence of life and when at last the descent could no longer be delayed I was met by the spreading aroma of frying bacon. A new day was beginning, waiting for me to join in, but I had the inescapable feeling that I had stolen an extra day from the early hours that follow the dawn. Place Fell had helped to bring one more dimension to an ever-widening experience of Lakeland's endless beauty.

GRANGE FELL
If you make Keswick your base for a walking holiday and fail to climb Grange Fell you miss the pleasure of wandering on one of the minor gems of the English Lake District.

It is easy to climb, but oh! so easy to miss out with all that glorious hinterland of Borrowdale within easy reach. Grange Fell may be minor in bulk, only a pimple when compared with the Scafells, Great Gable, Skiddaw and the rest, but a major share of nature's bounty has been set down in this tiny area, just waiting to please the senses of those discerning enough to realize its worth.

The fell is named from the village of Grange-in-Borrowdale which in turn takes its name from the days of Furness Abbey when that monastic order had its main farm—or grange—in the valley at that spot. It was, and still is, a key position below the narrows of the Jaws of Borrowdale and above the marshy delta at the head of Derwentwater. Grange Bridge spans the Derwent at the most obvious point and what more natural place could there be for a village to develop? The hamlet may have unwittingly made a fortunate choice by seating itself on the west bank, away from the busy Borrowdale road of the present day, but the scenic bridge is a blessing with a sting attached because it takes the secondary road round the lake between its cottages.

Just south of Grange the Jaws of Borrowdale tighten their hold on the valley's lifeline and there is barely enough room to spare for the road to squeeze through beside the river. I suppose this is one of the places that the poet Thomas Gray had in mind when he worried that any undue noise might bring an avalanche crashing about his ears. Two hundred years later you can approach the place for the first time and wonder if the road can possibly proceed much further. And I've seen folk cast an apprehensive glance aloft as though to satisfy themselves that no loose boulder is perched on the rim of the crag where the road engineers carved a way so that modern traffic can reach the dale's head.

Without Grange Fell the Jaws of Borrowdale would not exist. If the precipices of Castle Crag, to the west, are the upper incisors then their lower counterparts are the craggy bastions of this rugged little hill. King's How does its very best to bar the way, to seal the upper valley from prying eyes. The summit of King's How is a superb place for viewing the geography of upper Borrowdale. It is National Trust property, obtained and named in memory of King Edward VII, and no sovereign could have a better memorial than this jewel among Lakeland's hills. But it is not the highest point of the fell—that honour goes to Brund Fell. There are two more named tops, Ether Knott and Brown Dodd, but they are really high points along the north ridge. Brund Fell and King's How are the twin summits of Grange Fell but, though it is slightly lower, King's How deserves to be nominated as the summit supreme.

King's How is poised marvellously amid some of Lakeland's loveliest scenery. Southward is the peaceful green basin of Borrowdale—peaceful from here, anyway, for you don't notice the road and you can only guess at the traffic jams. Down there is a harmony of fields and trees that is not always present when man leaves his mark on the environment, and all around is a panorama of mountains, each a magnet in its own right but when you are on King's How you could hardly wish to be anywhere else. No one ever hurries on Grange Fell and King's How is particularly conducive to a prolonged halt. Just south of the top is a shelf of land ending in a rim of bare rock rather like the rim of a saucer. We once spent a fascinating half-hour there, turning over rocks and rendering homeless millions of ants. I've never seen so many ants in such close proximity. We were tempted into the fantasy of believing that we had discovered a new species—the Fell Walker Ant. But, fortunately for those enjoying their jam butties on the crest, they showed no propensity for indulging in peak-bagging.

All those stones were turned in the cause of cairn building, the only time I have had a hand in the initiation of a cairn. Really there are cairns in plenty on the fells but on that day in 1968 we felt the urge to mark the spot where you have the best of an outstanding outlook and the rim of rock gives more depth to the view than the summit of King's How. We had a willing workforce on hand to gather building material; an enthusiastic and cheerful group of primary school children full of youthful high spirits and overflowing with energy just waiting to be tapped and turned to some useful purpose. So apologies are due to those who frown on additional cairns. But ten years later it was still there in a very much modified form.

To the south-east of King's How is Brund Fell, bristling with chunks of rock both large and small, a scrambler's paradise. Of course there are other ways to reach Brund Fell, though none to equal the winding, carefree backdoor approach from King's How. The Rosthwaite-Watendlath track is barely half a mile distant. The direct route from Watendlath involves about a mile of walking, some of which can be decidedly wet, but it is best done in descent to have Watendlath in front as you go, tarn and cottages spread before you in a hidden hollow in the hills.

I have always liked Watendlath. In spite of its hackneyed reputation and the inevitable crowds of summer the place contrives to impress with a sense of the remote. Perhaps the visitors contribute to this feeling, for as you watch them pottering around, perhaps seeking evidences of Hugh Walpole's *Judith Paris*, you know that when the day is over they'll be gone and the contact with the outside world that they alone seem to bring will be severed.

The name is a curiosity. Now and then the old chestnut goes the rounds, that lisping honeymooners like to murmur "What endleth blith!" But learned authorities have a more sensible suggestion. Wath (a ford), tarn and lath (a barn) have existed since days of early settlement—perhaps a thousand years ago—and it is easy to see how these could be brought together to become the present name. Or in those early days the tarn belonged to a settler called Tundelau who had a homestead there. Water (or "vatn" in his tongue) of Tundelau could understandably evolve into Watendlath. But it hardly matters. Modern Watendlath, with or without the crowds, is a delightful hamlet in a lovely little dale with crags, trees, water and pastures, laced with the perennial stone walls of the north country.

I remember coming over the track from Watendlath to Stonethwaite a couple of days after one of Borrowdale's notorious floods and seeing walls, hedges and fences festooned with flood debris. A local man told me that his car had vanished but was found a couple of fields away. Already the pastures were dry and fresh in the pleasant summer sunshine but though the waters come and go quickly they leave more destruction in their wake than is comprehended by the ordinary visitor.

The flood waters are released from higher sources above the head of the dale. Grange Fell generally sails clear of the havoc, though flash floods have been recorded in Troutdale. But usually the fell is watered by Lakeland's gentler rains. Ringed by crags, girt with trees, it is a place for tranquil wanderings on the best of summer days—but its charms are captivating in any season. There are many places that can claim to be of outstanding beauty in this unique corner of England but that is a statement whose validity is as sure here as anywhere in the land.

HAYSTACKS

Haystacks is the epitome of the very best of Lakeland fell country. It is a mountain of contrasts. Though falling short of the 2,000-foot contour you can never call Haystacks a mere hill and the term "fell", accurate though it may be, seems hardly appropriate for so rugged a mass. For me it has always been a mountain and always will be. Darkly shadowed crags, a legacy of the last ice age of some 10,000 years ago, turn a grimly austere face to Buttermere—yet the summit plateau has been clothed by nature in a raiment of pleasant hues and textures. Given the right day and season this is a place for carefree wandering when the gentle hum of insects and the sparkle of standing water make it one of the most enchanting places imaginable.

I have read that Haystacks is one of those excellent "small hills" best reserved for a day when bad weather rules out the highest tops. Such treatment does it less than justice. Its many, varied delights can only be appreciated to the full on a sunny day in July when true summer slows the walker's pace and time is of no consequence. In fact, if the high tops are out of bounds, Haystacks certainly should be. It is no place to explore when mist threatens.

The opportunities for bringing a fell-walking career to a sudden and permanent conclusion are manifold.

I first visited the mountain on a walk along the Buttermere skyline from Fleetwith Pike to Red Pike. The sojourn on Haystacks was brief, but long enough for me to realize that here was a fell that positively demands far more than such hasty treatment. Later visits helped to redress the balance. There are memories of lunches taken sitting on rocky outcrops along the shore of Innominate Tarn with the summit lying across the water, patiently waiting for lazy footsteps to take us that way. Gentle strolls through sun-drenched heather have been accompanied by the serenade of industrious bees gathering a rich harvest of Haystacks' special honey. An eventual arrival at the summit rocks has brought once more that view of Buttermere with the distant buildings of Gatesgarth looking like a set of tiny dolls' houses in a bower of trees.

Of course Haystacks does have its fair share of Lakeland's wettest weather but for me it is the Sunshine Mountain. Perhaps I have been lucky—though probably not, because on Haystacks I try to choose my weather—but the worst I have ever suffered up there has been a stiff breeze and even that was tempered by the rays of a benevolent sun. And the breeze had its use in helping to dry out the clothes of one of our party when he made too close an acquaintance with the tarn.

Innominate Tarn is a splendid pool, one of a handful of top favourites. Small Water in its incomparable setting of corrie and cliff, Angle Tarn above Patterdale, tiny Lincombe Tarn on the ridge of Allen Crags, Loughrigg's little Lily Tarn—they are all of the best in their own different ways but on the right sort of day there is none I would exchange for Innominate Tarn. Nestling in a saucer-like bowl between a wide blue sky and the wide jumbled ridge of the mountain-top, it looks exactly how a mountain tarn should and is at its best when a gentle breeze raises triangles of lambent sunlight against the background of colourful heather and outcrops of warm, grey rock.

The main track across the summit plateau follows the northern margin of Innominate Tarn. This is the way to the summit when you climb from the depths of Warnscale Bottom or if you cross from Honister, and to reach it you pass the fell's largest mere, Blackbeck Tarn. This tarn— for me—is something of a disappointment, certainly less of an attraction and suffering in the inevitable comparison with Innominate Tarn. Perhaps it is away from the centre of things, or it may be that I always pass by in too much of a hurry, anxious for the choicer offerings ahead. The track crosses the outlet stream where the issuing waters purl their unsuspecting way towards the steep plunge of Black Beck bound for the senior mere from which the valley takes its name. I understand that a good scrambler's route is possible alongside Black Beck. I must try it some time. It looks steep and direct, offering fine opportunities for future exploration.

In addition to the two main tarns there are other pools scattered about the summit acres. One which cannot be passed without comment nestles in a rocky trough at the very top. There are other summit tarns in the district, notably on Red Screes, but this must be the finest. It makes a splendid foreground to views of the surrounding fells.

All these fells look good from Haystacks, as usually is the case when you look at a mountain from a lesser height. A pity Haystacks falls short of them in altitude—if it was a thousand feet higher it would rank with the best. That is a sentiment I have heard voiced more than once, but really it has no need to compete with its neighbours, Great Gable, Pillar, High Stile and the rest. By virtue of this lack of height it can claim something those noble fells can never show. You have only to stand on those summits to see what I mean. They are mountains that pay for their extra altitude. They must manage without the heather, the greenery and the tarns that give the top of Haystacks its individual and inimitable charm. If higher it would still be a rugged fell of great individuality but the special magic would be gone. No, Haystacks is better the way it is.

Perhaps the finest approach is from below the craggy Buttermere face where the valley ends in the steeps at the head of Warnscale Bottom. There is a choice of routes. Very popular is the Dubs Quarry "road" which makes its way round the lower slopes of Fleetwith Pike, but the old zigzags at the Haystacks side of Warnscale Beck are more interesting. These, too, are part of an ancient quarry way, a cunningly contrived track which is now of service to walkers bound for Haystacks by way of Blackbeck and Innominate Tarns. It is the connoisseur's way to the top.

We once introduced a group of children from industrial West Yorkshire to the Lakeland fells here. It was late July—as usual—and possibly the finest day of a superb summer. From the moment we left Gatesgarth everything in the world seemed right, but for me just one small incident made the whole outing worthwhile.

As we neared the top of the old zigzags one eleven-year-old boy stopped just ahead of me and turned to gaze at the retrospective view of Buttermere. As I came up to him I looked at his face. It eloquently spoke the thoughts he struggled to express.

"It's just like . . ." he began, then paused as he tried to find adequate words to say what he felt. "It's just like . . . a picture postcard!" Maybe not great imagery, but I knew what Terry meant. And he didn't know it but those few words made my day.

16

RING OUT THE OLD
(Lonely Fells at Swindale Head)

The last day of December—Silver Jubilee Year, 1977—
dawned damp and dull but I intended to ring out the old
year with a day on the fells and saw no reason for a change
of plan. It would be damp up there too, but dull—never! In
the eyes of the converted the fells are never dull. Quiet,
lonely, unexciting perhaps, but certainly not dull. Cynical
mortals may remain unconvinced and suggest that this is
just a matter of suiting the terminology to one's purpose.
However that may be, poor weather seems to make city
streets dull whereas on the hills it makes for a change of
scene and even familiar fells can show strange new facets,
so that you can have the feeling of treading new ground in
places that you should know like your own backyard. Mist,
rain or snow may cause modifications to plans but rarely
prevent me from reaching for the tops. If Sarah is involved
it is a different matter for you don't expose youngsters to
the worst vicissitudes of our climate; however, on this
occasion there was just myself to consider. I drove into
Swindale happy to cast aside the cares of a workaday
world, imaginary or otherwise.

I parked at Swindale Foot. The narrow valley road is
devoid of passing places and short of room for a parked car,
and there can be no sympathy for visitors who take the
paint off their precious vehicles in desperate manoeuvres
arising from confrontations with tractors and other traffic
which of necessity must rely on the lane for day to day
business. This is a working valley, in no way geared to the
needs of an influx of tourists, so it is only fair to leave the
road to those who use it for their livelihood. In any case
there is so much to see that is missed from a car window.
The couple of miles between Swindale Foot and Swindale

Head make a pleasant introduction to a shy valley if taken as a gentle walk—or do as I did and climb to the Mardale watershed leaving the winding lane till the day's end when you can return with a head full of thoughts about a quiet group of lonely fells where few strangers ever tread.

The fell tops round here have more in common with the Pennines away to the east than with Lakeland as we know it. Even the grassy Howgills seem to have more shape about them than Swindale's unexciting ridges, but the head of the dale is a different matter. There you will find a cirque of crags split by a fierce gully where Hobgrumble Gill becomes a perpendicular streak of white water as it drops from its secret little hanging valley on the verge of the skyline. Swindale's cliffs may not be large in the context of Lakeland generally but they look the part in this miniature setting. The small size of the valley makes them look much bigger than they really are—scenically the place is excellent, though any rock climber attracted by the hachures of the O.S. map could well come away disappointed. There are other crags in Swindale, notably the long dark line of Gouther and Outlaw Crags, on the right as you walk down-dale. Seen from the lane they have the sort of character that would make them look good in any company and one huge flake of rock seems impossibly glued to the upper half of a smooth, sheer precipice.

The nearest that most walkers get to Swindale is the head of Longsleddale when they seek to add a few outlying summits to their bag of Lakeland peaks. Grey Crag, Tarn Crag, Branstree and Selside Pike are the sort of fells that tend to be climbed just once, for the record, and in many ways that is all they deserve if it is just the summits you seek out. One cold, wintry day we came down from Tarn Crag to the wet col between the upper reaches of Mosedale and Longsleddale. The two of us had planned a circuit of the Longsleddale fells and Branstree should have been our next port of call. To say the least, it looked unappealing. Selside Brow appeared barren apart from its wall, reaching from top to bottom as straight and true as if it had been laid out by a paper-hanger with a plumb-line. It might have been totally without interest had we not noticed a group of red deer grazing half-way up the slope. We stopped awhile to watch them before turning away to Gatescarth Pass and Harter Fell. Not for the first time Branstree had lacked the magnetism to get us up there.

Branstree is that sort of hill, an outsider on the verge of Lakeland with no real distinction and probably only visited by determined peak-baggers who may never go that way again. It may fairly be described as a Mardale fell. Although it does lie exactly at the head of Longsleddale it is certainly more obvious from Mardale and has a substantial footing in the valley along the shore of Haweswater. Even so it is overshadowed by the grand ring of hills centred on High Street. Mardale is a fell walkers' dale but Branstree does not seem part of it, just an after-thought to turn your back on when you leave the car park and head for better things.

Longsleddale, too, is well enough endowed with fells and the inclusion of a grassy hill, even one of 2,333 feet, would add little to a fine dale head. South-east is Mosedale, wide and wet and lonely, with Mosedale Beck tracing a devious course well above the 1,000-foot contour before making an abrupt plunge into Swindale. You might say that Branstree is the mountain that nobody wants.

Branstree stands well back from all this as if in apology for being there at all. In fact only the latest metric maps admit the common usage and give the summit a name. It gets no mention on my one-inch Tourist Map where Artle Crag is the nearest name to the top. However, "Brant Street" appears half-way down the Mardale flank and it is clear that "Branstree" is a corruption of this. The newest map has dropped Brant Street altogether.

This could be a result of the most recent survey. An O.S. "ring" now adorns the highest point. Perhaps poor old Branstree is not considered worthy of a full-scale trigonometrical column—or is it just a matter of economy? Loadpot Hill, five miles away, gained a column at about the same time but Branstree must make do with a neat concrete circle at ground level. It does bear a proud inscription: "Ordnance Survey Trigonometrical Station". Rather a mouthful and just as forgettable as the summit itself.

Artle Crag is no more than a scattering of stones on the northern edge of the little plateau of a top. The best part of the mountain is low down on the Swindale side, those crags that close the valley head, but what you see is really part of Selside Pike, the next top along the ridge. This is where Mosedale Beck and Hobgrumble Gill make their sudden entries into Swindale and join forces to become Swindale Beck.

The cascades of Hobgrumble Gill shun close inspection. More easily seen at close quarters are Swindale Forces at the eastern end of the crags. There are not many waterfalls in the district that can claim equality with Swindale Forces. Few are better. Mosedale Beck plunges some 250 feet in a lateral distance of about 400 yards. The beck drops over a series of waterslides and cliffs to produce a spectacle that is absolutely typical of the best in Lakeland. The place is quite unsuspected until you are almost upon it and if your first approach is from above—as mine was—the sudden revelation is undeniably dramatic. After the indolent meanders of the beck in Mosedale this burst of activity comes as a shock even when you may be expecting something of the kind. The track linking Mosedale and Swindale keeps well away from the falls so you can quite easily miss them but those who know what they are looking for would never forgo the short detour east.

Rather than risk missing anything I followed the beck out of Mosedale. The flat floor of the upper valley narrows at the entrance and rocky knolls suggest an imminent change in character. Then, with hardly any preamble, the lazy stream quickens its pace and leaps joyfully into its most exciting quarter mile between source and sea. The shape of the ravine thrusts the sound of turmoil forward so that hardly a whisper reaches a walker in Mosedale until he is virtually on the lips of the cascades. After pausing a moment I dodged round an outcrop to emerge near the foot of the upper Force. A first impression was that there had hardly been enough water in Mosedale Beck to produce this kind of spectacle—not that Mosedale is exactly dry. There would appear to be sufficient water to keep a Niagara in business but mostly it seems content to stay where it is. Obviously it manages to percolate through the sodden peat and the evidence is there to see in Swindale Forces. Each variation on the theme of succeeding cascades can be reached by modest scrambles made necessary by the crags that are the cause of it all.

Lucky Swindale to have such a showpiece and yet be able to hide it away in a secluded corner. Fortunate again is the valley that came so near disaster in the form of a reservoir which was on the cards twenty years ago. In the event Manchester chose Wet Sleddale and that valley's loss is Swindale's gain. Water *is* taken from Swindale but the tiny dam and waterworks are unobtrusive enough to pass unnoticed unless you happen to be looking for them and the aqueduct that pipes the precious fluid to swell the Haweswater supply is tastefully hidden from view.

Mardale is a different matter but the story of that valley is well known. Branstree and Selside Pike sit aloof from all this though they form the crest of the watershed between two contrasting dales, one inundated by a reservoir, the other a little bit of the old Westmorland that in name is gone for ever except as a folk-memory that will persist. When I decided to ring out the old in Jubilee year these considerations made my choice of approach an easy one. It had to be Swindale. I went straight on to the fells from Swindale Foot to follow the watershed from Harper Hills.

This is a wide, gently undulating ridge. Some of the minor bumps are cairned and one of these, Hare Shaw, has achieved a modest distinction as a result of metrication. Its height is exactly 500 metres, no more, no less. It is faced by a tiny crag and marks the point at which the ridge begins to take a more definite course, where two separate ridges combine to form a unified watershed. North-east of Hare Shaw Mardale and Swindale are kept apart by the minor valley of Naddle. A glance into this little dale reveals a pleasant scene of easy, tree-clad slopes: the Naddle Forest, one of Lakeland's few relict woodlands. No marching files of conifers down there, but a natural treescape of oak, ash and birch. Swindale, too, has small patches of woodland that may well be a remnant of Cumbria's original tree-cover.

From Hare Shaw the slope is almost imperceptible for about half a mile then, after the slightest of depressions, comes a more marked rise leading to Selside Pike—the best summit on the ridge with a fine old cairn as shelter against the prevailing wind. Between Selside Pike and Branstree, on the Mardale side, is the wide grassy hollow of Hopgill Beck, overlooked by a fine beacon on Artlecrag Pike.

But on the nearby skyline is a rather more eye-catching construction, a strange sort of edifice that is one of the mysteries of the fells unless you have done your homework and know its history. A study of the O.S. map is an aid to comprehension. It is marked as a cairn. Usually the stylized lettering reserved for "cairn" is a sure indication of an antiquity but here the print is simple italic and that is rare enough to be of note. Simple cairns as the walker understands the term are largely ignored, which is hardly surprising in land where they must be numbered in their thousands. Their multiplicity and the ephemeral nature of so many of them mitigates against official recognition. (The 2½-inch map does acknowledge the presence of the more permanent examples, but with the rather prosaic title "pile of stones".)

In this area there are at least five examples in simple italic. Three of them—this on Branstree, one on Tarn Crag and another on the Great Howe ridge of Grey Crag—are almost in line, a line that can be extended north to Haweswater just where the extraction tower is placed. And that is the clue. These three "cairns" are of similar construction. They are redundant survey posts built by Manchester's waterworks engineers in conjunction with the laying of the aqueduct that now carries Lakeland's water out of the district. Their function forgotten they stand forlorn and, for me at least, they add to the solitude of these lonely hills of the eastern fringe.

I passed the survey post and crossed Branstree with a view of the High Street range, lined with snow along the ridge-top, but there were few long views on this last day of the year. The clouds were low and mist was an ever-present threat, and though it never settled long enough to pose any problems of navigation the high hills to the west played a game of hide-and-seek in the panorama.

As I followed the wall down Selside Brow the craggy upper reaches of Longsleddale filled with turbulent drifts of luminescent white vapour, a seething cumulus which bubbled up slowly, but as inevitably as milk boiling over the edge of pan before you can reach it. The eddies of cloud spilled over into Mosedale pushed by a gentle breeze, pointing the way ahead. Down Mosedale, past the banks of spoil that mark the old quarries, past the sheep pens and the lonely shepherds' bothie of Mosedale Cottage, and into the intimate dell that is Swindale; that was the way for me. There the rain caught up with me, an accompaniment along the final easy miles to transport home.

And so the year ended where the last had begun, in the hills—now Swindale, then the Howgill Fells. But there was another year around the corner and strangely my next hill proved to the The Calf. I was in the Howgills again. But as I drove home I knew nothing of that. There was just the thought of a year of promise ahead, a year of hills to climb and hills to explore, as there always will be as long as I have the strength to pull on a pair of boots and take to the fells.

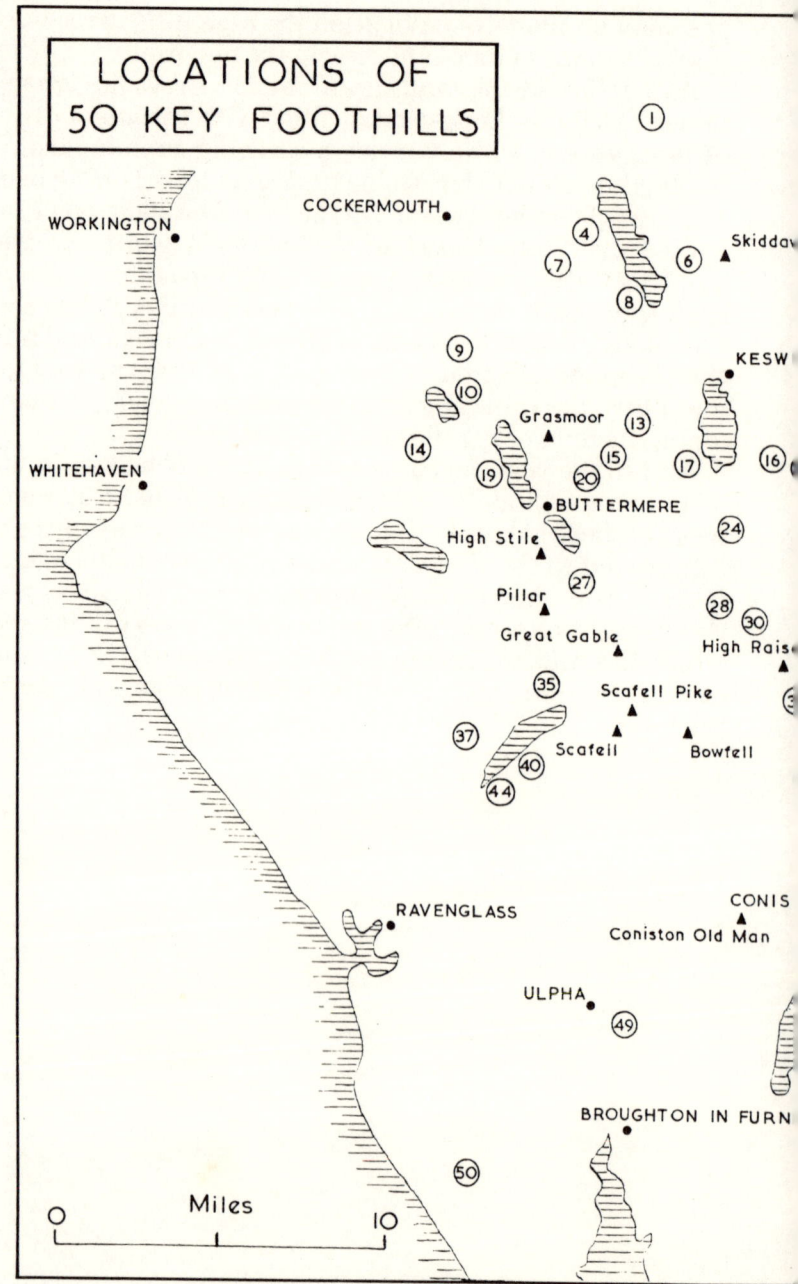

LOCATIONS OF
50 KEY FOOTHILLS

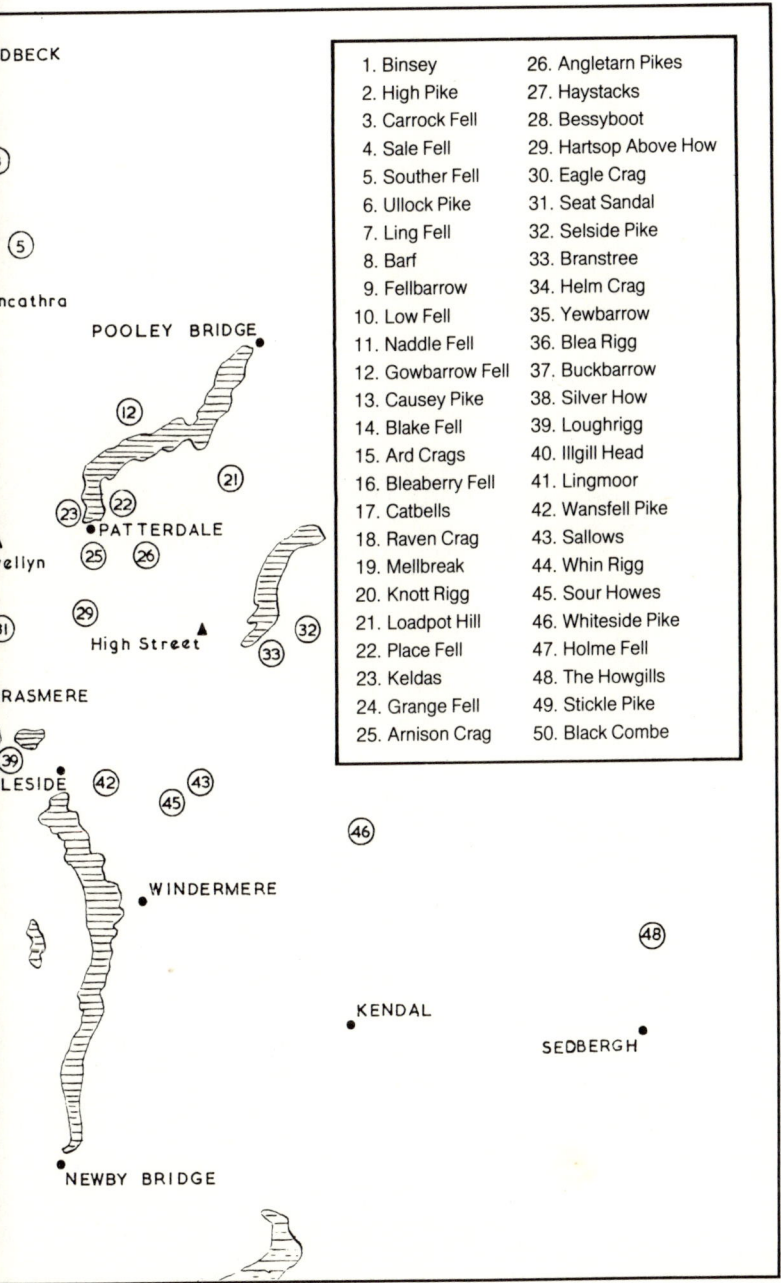

DBECK

(5)

ncathra

POOLEY BRIDGE

(12)

(21)

(23) (22)
PATTERDALE
(25) (26)
ellyn

(29)
High Street

(32)
(33)

RASMERE

(39)

LESIDE (42) (43)
(45)

(46)

WINDERMERE

(48)

KENDAL

SEDBERGH

NEWBY BRIDGE

1. Binsey	26. Angletarn Pikes
2. High Pike	27. Haystacks
3. Carrock Fell	28. Bessyboot
4. Sale Fell	29. Hartsop Above How
5. Souther Fell	30. Eagle Crag
6. Ullock Pike	31. Seat Sandal
7. Ling Fell	32. Selside Pike
8. Barf	33. Branstree
9. Fellbarrow	34. Helm Crag
10. Low Fell	35. Yewbarrow
11. Naddle Fell	36. Blea Rigg
12. Gowbarrow Fell	37. Buckbarrow
13. Causey Pike	38. Silver How
14. Blake Fell	39. Loughrigg
15. Ard Crags	40. Illgill Head
16. Bleaberry Fell	41. Lingmoor
17. Catbells	42. Wansfell Pike
18. Raven Crag	43. Sallows
19. Mellbreak	44. Whin Rigg
20. Knott Rigg	45. Sour Howes
21. Loadpot Hill	46. Whiteside Pike
22. Place Fell	47. Holme Fell
23. Keldas	48. The Howgills
24. Grange Fell	49. Stickle Pike
25. Arnison Crag	50. Black Combe

Index

Mosedale Beck (Swindale), 193, 194
Mosedale Beck (Wasdale), 118
Mosedale Cottage, 197
Mosedale Horseshoe, 95
Moser, 159
Mosser, 71
Mosser Beck, 73
Mosser Lane, 69
Mousthwaite Col, 164
Mousthwaite Combe, 163
Mungrisdale, 162, 163
Mungrisdale Common, 21

Nab Scar, 143
Naddle Beck, 109
Naddle Fell, 109–12
Naddle Forest, 195
Naddle Valley (Mardale), 195
Naddle Valley (Thirlmere), 110
Nameless Fell, 149
National Trust, 185
Nether Row, 52, 53
Nethermost Cove, 144
Nethermost Pike, 54, 144
Newlands, 21, 40, 42, 56, 58, 87, 89, 90
Newlands Fells, 79
Newlands Hause, 55, 56, 57, 89

Oak Howe Needle, 105
One Man and his Dog, 70
Ore Gap, 127
Outerside, 90
Outlaw Crag, 192
Over Beck, 97

Paper Moss, 112
Pardshaw, 71
Parkend Beck, 48, 49
Patterdale, 35, 36, 63, 144, 149
Peel, John, 43, 166
Pele, The, 133
Pennines, 60, 115, 152, 162, 170
Penrith, 161
Pike o'Blisco, 102
Pillar, 92, 96
Pillar Rock, 96, 103

Pillar Round, the, 95
Place Fell, 133, 181–3
Potter, Beatrix, 40
Potts Gill Mine, 50

Qualification for inclusion, 12

Raise Beck, 63, 64
Raise Gill, 170
Randygill Top, 18
Raven Crag (Helm Crag), 139, 140
Raven Crag (Thirlmere), 125, 171–2
Raven Crag (Yewdale), 113
Rawthey, River, 19, 22
Rawthey Valley, 21
Red Bank, 106, 178
Red Gill Beck, 16, 20
Red Pike (Buttermere), 76, 112, 188
Red Screes, 189
Rigg Beck, 55, 56, 57, 89
Robin Tarn, 179
Robinson, 42, 56, 57
Robinson's Cairn, 96
Rosthwaite, 86, 126
Rosthwaite Cam, 86–7
Rosthwaite Fell, 85–7, 130
Rothay Valley, 33
Roughton Gill, 48–9
Roughton Gill Mines, 49
Rowling End, 90, 91
Ruthwaite, 166
Ruthwaite Cove, 144
Rydal Water, 37, 38

Saddleback (see also Blencathra), 161
Sadgill, 158
Sail Beck, 55, 56
St John's Beck, 109
St John's-in-the-Vale, 110
St Patrick, 149
St Patrick's Well, 149
St Sunday Crag, 145, 146, 147
Sale Fell, 28, 65, 66, 67
Sallows, 58, 59